WHAT THE ACTUAL FUSS

Why the CX Buzzword Is Relentlessly Haunting You

Bibi Sofowote

Copyright © 2024 Bibi Sofowote
All rights reserved

No part of this book may be reproduced, or stored in a retrieval system, or transmitted in any form or by any means, electronic, mechanical, photocopying, recording, or otherwise, without express written permission of the publisher.

Dedication 16

Prologue 18

What Is Customer Experience, Really? .. 20

Zappos: A CX Masterclass 21

The Secret Behind the Magic: It's Not Magic 22

Why CX Matters Now More Than Ever ... 23

A Message for Dad (and Others Who Might Be Wondering) 24

Chapter 1 | Welcome to the CX Jungle 25

From Cave Paintings to Yelp Reviews 25

Your Customers Aren't Just Customers: Meet Your New BFFs 27

The CX Ecosystem: More Complex Than Your Last Relationship 29

Chapter 2 | The Science of CX: Yes, There's Math Involved 33

The Psychology of Customers: Why They Do What They Do (And Why You Should Care) 33

Data-Driven Decisions: How to Make Numbers Your (Other) New BFF 35

The Art of Listening: Eavesdropping on Your Customers (Legally) 37

Chapter 3 | Designing a Beautiful Customer Experience Is the Blueprint for Success 41

Mapping the Customer Journey: It's Not Just a Sunday Drive 41

Touchpoints Galore: Creating Moments That Matter (And Avoiding Awkward Silences) 43

Building a Customer-Centric Culture: It's Like Herding Cats, But Worth It 46

Chapter 4 | The Secret Sauce of Customer Engagement: It's Not Ketchup 49

Personalization, Because Nobody Wants to Feel Like a Number 49

Omnichannel Strategies: Meeting Customers Where They Are (Even in Their PJs) 51

The Power of Storytelling: How to Turn Customers into Raving Fans 53

Chapter 5 | Metrics That Matter: Measuring Customer Experience Without Losing Your Mind.................. 56

KPIs: Key Performance Indicators or Keeping People Irritated? 56

NPS, CSAT, and Other Acronyms: Decoding the Customer Experience Language 58

The Feedback Loop: How to Ask for Feedback Without Sounding Desperate . 60

Chapter 6 | The Future of CX: Trends That Will Make You Go "Hmmm" 63

AI and Automation: Your New Customer Service Co-Workers 63

The Rise of the Experience Economy: When Experiences Are Worth More Than Stuff 65

Sustainability: Why Your Customers Want You to Save the Planet (And How to Do It) 67

Chapter 7 | Crafting Connections: Real-Life CX Stories Worth Your Attention . 71

Brands That Nailed It: CX Wins You'll Want to Copy 71

Lessons from the Trenches: What Not to Do 73

The Customer Experience Revolution: Join or Get Left Behind 76

Chapter 8 | Putting It All Together: Your Action Plan for CX Success 79

Developing a Customer Experience Strategy: Your Roadmap to Greatness ... 79

Building a Customer Experience Team: Assembling Your Avengers 81

Continuous Improvement: Because Perfection is Just a Myth (But We Can Try) 83

Chapter 9 | Rolling with the Punches: The Art of Staying Relevant 86

The Importance of Adaptability: Change is the Only Constant (And In-Laws... Change and In-Laws) 86

Celebrating Your Wins: Because Who Doesn't Love a Good Party? 88

Staying Curious: The Key to Long-Term Success (And Lifelong Learning) 90

Chapter 10 | Reinforcing Some Ideas: Prioritize CX Leadership 93

Do It Right or Don't Bother 93

Why CX Should Be a Priority 94

The Netflix Lesson: Lagging Indicators Are Just That – Lagging 95

CX Leadership Needs to Be at the Table 96

Why CX Leaders Need Authority and Influence 97

The Stakes Are Higher Than Ever 97
Don't Cook CX on the Back Burner 98
Chapter 11 | A Closer Look at NPS (And What You Should Really Know) 99
Think Fast! What's NPS? 99
NPS: The Basics 100
When NPS Goes Wrong: The Spiffy Lube Disaster 101
The Dangers of Misusing NPS 102
The Complexities of Customer Feedback 103
What Spiffy Lube Learned (The Hard Way) 104
The Moral of the Story: Use NPS, But Don't Let It Use You 105
Chapter 12 | Securing Stakeholder Allyship, Because Even Superman Is Part of a League 107
Don't Get Stuck Going Nowhere Fast ... 107
When CX Is Not a Priority (Yet) 108

WIIFM: What's In It For Me? 108

Back It Up with Data (Leave the Inspirational Speeches at Home) 110

Identify Your Champions 111

Make Them Part of the Solution 111

The Bottom Line: CX Requires Collective Ownership 112

Chapter 13 | EX & CX From 30,000ft, Without the Vertigo 114

Are Employees Really a Big Deal? 114

The Employee-Customer Connection: What Branson Knows That Many Don't 115

Why Employee Experience (EX) Matters to CX 116

Maslow's Hierarchy, But for Employees 117

The Three Environments That Impact EX
.... 118

The Cost of Ignoring EX 119

You Can't Give What You Don't Have .. 120

The Bottom Line: EX Drives CX 120

Chapter 14 | CX Operations & CX Engagement: The Property Brothers Or Jekyll & Hyde? **122**

A Package Deal for Success 122

CX Engagement: The Emotional Connection 123

CX Operations: The Engine That Powers Engagement 124

The Symbiotic Relationship: Engagement Informs Operations 125

Consistency Is King 126

The Property Brothers of CX: Engagement & Operations Working Together 126

Chapter 15 | Change Management for Adopting Customer-Centricity (Part 1) **128**

The Struggle of Change – Even When It's Good 128

So, What Is Customer-Centricity, Really? 129

The Pain of Changing Mindsets 131

Tools and Processes: Fit for Purpose or Cramping Style?................................. 131

The Game-Changer: Change Management 132

The Perils of Not Having a Plan 133

The Road Ahead 133

Chapter 16 | Change Management for Adopting Customer-Centricity (Part 2) 135

Mapping Out a Plan of Action: From Ideas to Results 135

1. Establish the Need for Change 136

2. Articulate the Vision for a Customer-Centric Future.. 136

3. Align the Organization Behind the Vision 137

4. Identify Stakeholders and Overcome Resistance 138

5. Develop Skills and Implement New Tools 138

6. Maintain Consistency and Measure Progress 139

7. Risk Mitigation: Navigating the Hurdles 140

8. Celebrate Successes Along the Way 140

In Closing: A Launchpad for Transformation 141

Chapter 17 | Distinguishing Customer Success from Customer Experience. 143

Similar, But Not the Same 143

Understanding Customer Success 144

Defining Customer Experience 145

Where They Intersect: The Synergy of Success and Experience 146

The Functional vs. Emotional Divide 147

Building a Customer-Centric Strategy with Both CX and CS 148

The Value of a Holistic Approach 149

Chapter 18 | Wrapping It Up: What the Fuss Is Really All About 151

You Made It! 151

CX Is More Than Just a Department; It's a Philosophy 151

Success and Experience Go Hand in Hand 152

Change Management: The Key to Becoming Truly Customer-Centric 152

Consistency, Feedback, and Continuous Improvement: The Lifeblood of CX 153

Taking Care of Your Team So They Can Take Care of Your Customers 153

So, Why Does the CX Buzzword Relentlessly Haunt Us? 154

Keep Striving for Customer Excellence. 154

Glossary **157**

About the Author **167**

Dedication

October 2024. I dedicate this book to my wife Ona, and to our two little daughters, Sage and Aria, the older of whom is now at an age where we're having a great time constantly answering a slew of "why" questions. This book couldn't exist without their love and support.

This is also a great opportunity to highlight the kindness and encouragement I have always been able to count on from my sister, Lorade, my brothers, Wande and Yemi, our dad, Segun, and constantly in my heart and spirit, my dearly departed mother, Funke.

I would also like to say big thanks to a few of the people who have been truly impactful in my career in general, and in this exhilarating journey of Customer Experience execution, management and leadership in particular. In no particular order, they are Tracy Gelder, Joe Anderson, Etiene Etukudoh, Jeff McEachern, Andrea Clarke-Thompson, Tunji Akintokun, and Mbula Munyao-Sang (who sadly is no longer here with us, but whose influence continues to be invaluable as I go through professional life and leadership).

Finally, I would like to acknowledge all the friends and acquaintances from within my professional network who took the time to interact with and share feedback on the CX-focused series of podcast episodes, newsletter editions and vlogs that formed the basis of this book.

Prologue
The Elevator Pitch, Executive Summary or Last-minute Book Report

When in 2023, I began to put out Customer Experience focused content, it wasn't long before I began to get a few nudges, some sincere, others jocular, about writing a book.

"But there are already so many books!" I said. "What could *I* possibly add to the shelf to make the effort worth it?"

But after a while, I started to take a different kind of look at my posts, and realized that almost invariably, the feedback was some version of "You took this topic and made it so easy to understand with your wit and humor". Wit and humor, me? Stop it, I like it!

The truth is, I've always learned best when humor was applied. My favorite teachers through school and life have always been those who were able to take a complex concept and bring it all the way down to what I'm convinced is my very average intellectual capacity. Therefore, when I started to put out CX content, I thought I'd do it in a way that would appeal to an audience of one: me. After all, there was no guarantee that anyone but myself would care enough to check it out.

And now that I've decided to grab the quill and write a book, I'm taking the same approach. This book is irreverent and intentionally devoid of academic stuffiness. It may not come up to the high and exacting standards of professorial work, but I'll be damned if you don't have a good time reading and learning. The book has even been accused of inducing a laugh-out-loud moment from time to time, and for that, I willfully refuse to apologize.

When you tell people that you work in Customer Experience, they probably have a lot of questions. Some might even feel awkward about asking them. You see it in their eyes. They nod along, they smile politely, but you know, deep down, they have no idea what CX actually is. And to be honest, you don't blame them. Customer Experience is one of those corporate buzzwords that floats around the room like a trendy new diet everyone's trying, but no one fully understands. But if you think that's bad, try explaining it to your dad.

Now, I'd like to think my dad is proud of me. He knows I do important work. But here's the thing: I'm pretty sure he has no idea what it is that I do. It's not that he's out of touch. For a man in his late 80s, he's surprisingly tech-savvy. In fact, we recently had to stage a little family intervention to get him to use his computer *less*. He's always on there, writing, doing creative work, hopping on video calls with his grand-babies on the weekends. The geographical divide between Germany and Canada doesn't faze him one bit. He's connected. But despite all that, every week, when he asks how work is going, I know for a fact that when I give my response, he's satisfied, but utterly clueless.

And if my dad doesn't get what I do, there's a good chance that a lot of other people don't either.

So, if you're like my dad, or perhaps someone else you know has dropped the term "Customer Experience" at dinner and you politely changed the subject to something easier, like the weather, this book is for you.

What Is Customer Experience, Really?

Let's get one thing out of the way: CX is not just about customer support or dealing with complaints. It's not limited to handling calls when someone's package gets lost or their internet goes down. Sure, that's part of it, but CX is much broader than that. Customer Experience is about the sum total of every interaction a customer has with your company. It's about how they feel when they browse your website, call your help center, or receive that long-awaited package. It's the culmination of moments, big and small, that shape the customer's perception of your brand.

Here's a straightforward way to put it:

Customer Experience is making sure that your customers get exactly what they need from you, exactly how they expect to receive it, or better.

Simple, right? Strip away all the jargon, the metrics, the KPIs, and that's what you're left with. CX is the discipline of making sure no one else does it better than you when it comes to delivering what your customers want. It's about making sure you're not just meeting customer expectations, you're exceeding them.

But let's not leave it there. Let's take a real-world example.

Zappos: A CX Masterclass

One company that has made CX its entire identity is Zappos. You may have heard of them. They're an online shoe and clothing retailer based in Nevada. But they're not just known for shoes; they're known for their Customer Experience. Their philosophy is simple: "Wow" the customer.

At Zappos, they don't just try to meet customer expectations, they shatter them. Employees are encouraged to go above and beyond, even if it means doing things that sound crazy to most companies. For example, Zappos allows customers to return items for any reason, no questions asked. They'll even give refunds when a customer technically isn't entitled to one. To most businesspeople, that sounds like a recipe for disaster. How can you build a sustainable business by bending over backwards for every single customer?

But here's the thing: Zappos understands that you can't go wrong when you take care of your customers. By prioritizing the customer's experience over short-term gains, they build loyalty. Customers know that when they shop with Zappos, they're in good hands. They'll be treated well. And because of that, they keep coming back, time and time again.

The Secret Behind the Magic: It's Not Magic

Now, before you start thinking that this level of Customer Experience is just some magical byproduct of fairy dust, let me stop you right there. Delivering this kind of CX doesn't happen by accident, and it certainly doesn't happen through sheer willpower. No, this is a calculated, well-executed strategy powered by a few key things: discipline, focus, execution, and leadership.

You see, Zappos' secret isn't just having nice employees. It's that they have built systems, processes, and a company culture that supports those employees. Every decision is driven by deep customer insights. Zappos knows what their customers want because they've invested in learning everything they can about them. They use data, feedback, and intuition to ensure that their CX efforts align with the things their customers care about most. It's not magic, it's a strategy. One that takes a lot of work.

And here's the kicker: they do it because they know that in today's hyper-competitive business world, the company that delivers the best value to the customer wins. It's that simple.

Why CX Matters Now More Than Ever

You don't need to be a genius to see that the business landscape has changed. Gone are the days when simply having a good product was enough. Customers have more options than ever before, and they know it. If you're not giving them an exceptional experience, there's always someone else who will. And that, in a nutshell, is why today, every corporate LinkedIn post, company keynote address, annual CEO report and product launch seems to include the word "Customer Experience", or "CX", just waiting to jump out at you.

Think of CX like running a large marathon event. There are dozens, maybe hundreds, of other runners vying for the same prize: the customer's loyalty. And in that race, the company that consistently delivers a better experience than the competition is the one that customers stick with. They renew, they repurchase, they recommend you to their friends.

So, if you're serious about growing your business, you need to be serious about Customer Experience.

A Message for Dad (and Others Who Might Be Wondering)

So there you have it: a highly condensed introduction to Customer Experience. And Dad, if for some reason you're reading this, I hope it clears things up. Now you can finally explain to all your friends what it is I do for a living. It's more than just emails and meetings, it's about making people happy. And what's better than that?

Customer Experience isn't just a buzzword. It's not a trendy topic that's going to fade into oblivion like shoulder pads or Blockbuster rentals. It's a business philosophy that, when done right, leads to loyal customers, sustainable growth, and a thriving company culture.

So, the next time someone asks you what CX is, you won't have to awkwardly change the subject to the weather. You can confidently tell them that CX is the future of business, and you're at the forefront of it.

Chapter 1 | Welcome to the CX Jungle

From Cave Paintings to Yelp Reviews

The journey of Customer Experience (CX) is as old as humanity itself, tracing back to our ancestors huddled around flickering fires, trying to make sense of the world through their rudimentary cave paintings. Imagine the first caveman, armed with nothing but a sharp implement and a penchant for storytelling, trying to impress his roommates with a visual account of his last mammoth hunt. Little did he know, he was laying the groundwork for what would eventually evolve into customer feedback and experience. "I had a great time hunting today," he might have exclaimed, while others nodded in agreement. Or, "That mammoth steak was a bit tough; I'd rate it a three out of five!" And just like that, the first customer surveys were born, albeit on rocky foundations.

Fast forward several millennia, and the complexities of Customer Experience have transformed dramatically. Gone are the days of deciphering cave drawings; today, customer feedback comes in the form of Yelp reviews and social media rants. Instead of grunting and gesturing, customers are now equipped with smartphones and Wi-Fi, ready to unleash their thoughts about your business faster than a cheetah on roller-skates. The once-vague concept of customer experience has morphed into a science, with analytics and metrics replacing cave walls. Metrics like Net Promoter Score (NPS) have become the new hieroglyphics, deciphered by professionals who would rather not be confronted by their own Yelp reviews.

As business leaders and entrepreneurs navigate this bustling landscape of customer expectations, they often find themselves in a comedic play – think Shakespeare meets Silicon Valley. One moment, they are the valiant knights, slaying the dragons of poor feedback; the next, they are the bumbling fools, tripping over their own customer service snafus. The quest for the holy grail of customer satisfaction is both noble and ridiculous, filled with plot twists that even the best sitcom writers would struggle to script. Each interaction is a scene, and every customer a potential critic ready to take to the stage of social media.

Now, let's not forget the role of technology in this evolving saga. The rise of Artificial Intelligence (AI) and machine learning is akin to introducing a wizard to the story. Suddenly, customer insights can be conjured up in mere seconds. However, with great power comes great responsibility, and business leaders must wield their data analytics tools wisely lest they become the cavemen of Customer Experience, misinterpreting trends and leading their teams into the wilderness of confusion. Customers are savvy, and they can spot a poorly-executed strategy from a mile away, like a cave bro sniffing out a week-old mammoth pie, even though the sign clearly said "Pies baked fresh daily".

In this comedic yet enlightening odyssey, the birth of Customer Experience as a business concept reminds us that the journey to excellence is far from over. As we navigate the choppy waters of feedback, reviews, and metrics, understanding the evolution from cave paintings to digital platforms is crucial. The playful nature of this transformation offers valuable lessons for all business professionals, reminding us that at the heart of Customer Experience lies not just data and strategy, but also a touch of humor and humanity. After all, whether it's a cave painting or a Yelp review, the goal remains the same: to connect, engage, and create experiences worthy of a five-star rating.

Your Customers Aren't Just Customers: Meet Your New BFFs

In the wild world of business, it's easy to think of customers as mere transaction machines, spitting out dollars in exchange for goods and services. But let's take a moment to consider a different perspective: what if your customers are more like that quirky friend who shows up at your door with a pizza and a movie, ready to make your day infinitely more interesting? Sure, you may not be besties right away, but if you play your cards right, they can transform from faceless buyers into your biggest cheerleaders. Just like that friend, your customers crave connection, understanding, and a sprinkle of fun in their interactions with you.

Picture this: you walk into a coffee shop where the barista knows your name, your favorite drink, and even your dog's name. Suddenly, that caffeine fix feels less like a transaction and more like a warm hug. Customers want that level of personal connection, too. They want to feel like they matter, not just to the bottom line but to you as a person... well, as much of a person as you can be through whatever channel you're interacting on. By taking the time to learn about your customers, you can turn them into loyal advocates who bring their friends along for the ride, just like that friend who insists you try their favorite pizza place because "It's the best!"

Now, let's not forget the power of a good laugh. Humor is like a secret sauce in Customer Experience. It can lighten the mood and create memorable interactions that customers will reminisce about long after they've left your store, or your website. Imagine sending a cheeky email that says, "We miss you more than our morning coffee!" or a social media post that pokes fun at the typical Monday blues. When customers see your brand's human side, they're not just buying a product; they're joining a community where laughter is encouraged, and people genuinely care. Who wouldn't want to stick around for that? I urge you to take a look at Duolingo's LinkedIn and other socials. Masterfully delivered hilarity driving home important communication.

Moreover, the friendships you forge with your customers can yield some serious business benefits. Think about it: loyal customers are like walking billboards, advertising your business to anyone who will listen. They'll rave about your product like a proud parent at a kindergarten graduation. When you treat customers like friends, they'll return the favor by spreading the word, sharing reviews, and maybe even bringing their friends along for a little shopping spree. The more you invest in these relationships, the more you'll find that your customer base is not just a group of buyers but a thriving network of advocates who are thrilled to support you.

In the end, embracing the idea that your customers can be your new best friends isn't just a feel-good mantra; it's a smart business strategy. By fostering genuine connections, sprinkling in some humor, and treating customers with the same care you'd give to your closest pals, you'll create an experience that goes beyond the transactional. So go on, open your doors wide, and welcome your customers into the fold. You might just find that the best friendships, and the best business results, come from a little kindness and a lot of laughs.

The CX Ecosystem: More Complex Than Your Last Relationship

Within the grand theater of business, the Customer Experience ecosystem resembles a complicated love life, complete with misunderstandings, unexpected plot twists, and the occasional dramatic exit. Shonda Rhimes would be proud. Just as in relationships, where one misstep can lead to the cold shoulder, a single miscalculation in Customer Experience can send your clientele running for the hills, or into the arms of smooth-talking Jim, who's just been waiting for the chance to step in with that irresistible small-town charm.

Imagine your customer as a romantic partner who has high expectations. You may think you know what they want, but just like that last date who claimed to be "totally cool with anything" while secretly judging your choice of restaurant, your customers have layers of preferences and emotions that can be quite the puzzle.

Navigating the customer experience landscape is akin to steering through a maze, where every turn presents a new challenge that requires finesse and strategy. One moment, you think you've aced the situation with a stellar product launch, and the next, your customers are ghosting you like a bad Tinder match after discovering you don't offer free returns, or that your profile picture is at least 10 years past expiration. The key to success lies in understanding that this ecosystem is not a straight line but a web of interactions, emotions, and expectations. It's about creating a harmony that resonates with your audience – a symphony of touchpoints that makes them feel like they are the stars of the show, not just background characters in your corporate drama.

Metrics and analytics in customer experience can feel like deciphering a cryptic love letter written in a foreign language. You've got your Net Promoter Score (NPS), Customer Satisfaction (CSAT)Score, and a host of other acronyms that could rival a high school chemistry exam. But remember, numbers alone won't win your customers' hearts; it's the story behind those numbers that counts. When you dive deep into the analytics, it's like reading between the lines of that love letter. You must interpret the signals, understand the patterns, and ultimately gain insights that help you tailor experiences that resonate on a personal level.

Moreover, just like relationships, the CX ecosystem thrives on communication. A well-timed follow-up is akin to sending a "Hey, how's it going?" text to a friend after a fun outing. It shows that you care, and it keeps the connection alive. On the flip side, neglecting this aspect can lead to the dreaded "seen but not responded" scenario. Customers today expect transparency and engagement, and if they feel ignored, they'll likely take their business (and their loyalty) elsewhere. So, keep those lines of communication open and make your customers feel like they're in a loving, committed relationship with your business, not just a casual fling.

Ultimately, crafting a successful customer experience is like writing a romantic comedy – there needs to be tension, resolution, and above all, a happy ending. Think P.G. Wodehouse. You want your customers to laugh, cry, and root for your business every step of the way. In this complex ecosystem, the goal is not just to meet expectations but to exceed them, leaving your customers feeling valued and appreciated.

So, take a page from the relationship playbook: treat your customers with kindness, listen to their needs, and above all, make them feel special. If you can do that, you'll not only keep them coming back for more, but you'll also create a bond that can weather (almost) any storm, just like a true love story.

Chapter 2 | The Science of CX: Yes, There's Math Involved

The Psychology of Customers: Why They Do What They Do (And Why You Should Care)

Understanding the psychology of customers is like trying to decipher a cat's behavior: just when you think you've figured it out, they surprise you by knocking something off your desk for no apparent reason. Customers are unpredictable, and their decisions can seem as random as a toddler's dance moves. However, beneath this chaotic surface lies a complex web of motivations, emotions, and experiences that drive their choices. As business leaders and entrepreneurs, it's crucial to tap into this psychological goldmine to craft unforgettable customer experiences.

Let's face it: customers are not always rational beings (just don't tell them I told you this). They can be swayed by their emotions quicker than a squirrel on caffeine. One moment they are loyal fans of your brand, and the next, they're flirting with your competitor because they posted a cute cat meme. Understanding the emotional triggers that lead to such spontaneous decisions can help you create marketing strategies that resonate. If you can mindfully and demurely tap into the joy of a well-timed pun or the nostalgia of a '90s throwback, you might just find yourself with a new customer who feels like they've known you forever. Like an old friend, minus the awkward silence.

Then there's the matter of social influence. Customers are always following trends and fads with varying degrees of enthusiasm. One viral TikTok dance, and suddenly 1 million people want your product, regardless of whether it's actually useful or not. Recognizing the power of social platforms can help you turn casual browsers into loyal buyers. If your product has been endorsed by a celebrity or appears in a viral video, customers could flock to you like seagulls to a dropped French fry. So, embrace the chaos and leverage social dynamics to your advantage. Just don't forget to keep an eye on your fries.

In addition to emotions and social influence, the need for convenience plays a starring role in customer psychology. Today's customers are busier than a one-armed juggler. If your product or service is not easily accessible, you might as well be selling ice to penguins. Streamlining the customer journey is essential. If it takes more than three clicks to buy your product, you may want to rethink your CX. Customers want speed, efficiency, and a sprinkle of delight. Make their lives easier, and they'll reward you with their loyalty; plus, a five-star review that could make you blush.

Finally, let's talk about the importance of feedback. Customers love to share their opinions, whether it's through social media rants or official reviews. They want to feel heard, like they're part of an exclusive club where only the most insightful critiques matter. Ignoring their feedback is like ignoring a toddler's tantrum. It's going to escalate quickly.

Engage with your customers, ask for their thoughts, and show that you value their input. It's not just about selling; it's about creating a connection. When customers feel valued, they're more likely to return, bringing their friends and a few extra bucks along for the ride. So, embrace the humor and chaos of customer psychology; it's a wild ride that can lead to fantastic business opportunities.

Data-Driven Decisions: How to Make Numbers Your (Other) New BFF

Data-driven decisions might sound like something only an android would get excited about, but fear not! Embracing the world of numbers doesn't mean you have to ditch your sense of humor or your love for spontaneous office dance parties. Think of data as that eccentric friend who always has a wealth of intriguing stories to share. Yes, they might seem a bit odd at first, but once you get to know them, you'll find they have the power to transform your Customer Experience game. So, let's dive into how numbers can become your new best friend forever, or at least until the next big trend comes along.

First things first, you need to understand that data is not just a bunch of random digits floating around like lost socks in a dryer. It's the lifeblood of your business decisions.

Imagine if you could predict customer behavior with the same accuracy as predicting the weather (or at least the likelihood of rain during your picnic). By harnessing customer metrics and analytics, you can uncover insights that would make Sherlock Holmes jealous. Whether it's tracking customer satisfaction scores or analyzing purchasing patterns, these numbers help you anticipate what your customers crave, even before they realize it themselves. Who knew being a mind reader could be this easy? Your Vegas residency awaits.

Now, let's talk about the actual process of making data your BFF. It's not as complicated as you might think. Start by identifying the key metrics that matter to your business. This could be anything from Net Promoter Score (NPS) to the average time it takes for a customer to find their favorite product on your website. Once you've pinpointed these metrics, treat them like your favorite Netflix series: binge-watch them regularly. Dive deep into the numbers, look for trends, and don't be afraid to pause and ask yourself, "What on earth does this mean?" Trust me, those "aha!" moments are often accompanied by a dramatic soundtrack in your head.

But wait, there's more! Making data-driven decisions isn't just about looking at numbers and saying, "Yup, that looks good." It's about weaving these insights into your Customer Experience strategy like a skilled artisan working to complete a bulk order from their Etsy store. Use the data to craft personalized experiences that make your customers feel like they've just stepped into a five-star hotel, even if it's just a simple interaction with your business. After all, who doesn't love being treated like royalty? By leveraging the power of data, you can create experiences that delight your customers and keep them coming back for more, like a favorite dessert they can't resist. There's this Ben & Jerry's peanut butter ice cream that I think might be a bit of a problem for me. I'm working on it. Pray for me.

Finally, let's not forget the importance of sharing your newfound love for data with your team. After all, it takes a village to raise a CX strategy, and your numbers should be the star of the show. Organize fun data parties... yes, you can totally have snacks and drinks while discussing metrics! Encourage your team to brainstorm based on the insights you've gathered. With everyone on board, you'll foster a culture where data isn't just a boring subject, but an exciting adventure that leads to extraordinary customer experiences. So go ahead, make those numbers your new BFF, and watch as they transform your business into a Customer Experience powerhouse!

The Art of Listening: Eavesdropping on Your Customers (Legally)

At the Renaissance Tour concert of Customer Experience, listening is your VIP backstage pass. You see, while many businesses are busy shouting their marketing messages from the rooftops, the real magic happens when you put your ear to the ground and tune in to what your customers are whispering, *legally*. Everyone heard me say "legally", right? I will *not* be sitting in on anyone's court hearing, just to be clear.

Think of it as listening in on a conversation between your customers and their inner selves. Sure, you won't be hiding behind the potted plant in the corner, or sneaking around like the persistent villain of The Perils of Penelope Pitstop. Showing my age a little there, but hey, there were reruns through the '90s! However, you *will* be gathering insights that are pure gold. After all, who doesn't want to know what their customers really think, especially when they're not on company time?

Now, you might be wondering how to engage in this art of listening without crossing any ethical lines. Worry not! The Internet is a treasure trove of customer feedback, from social media rants to product reviews, and you don't need a secret decoder ring to access it. Just an internet connection and you can be the Sherlock Holmes of customer insights; the deerstalker hat and pipe are optional. Dive into those online conversations, read between the lines, and uncover the gems of information that will help you craft a customer experience that's not just satisfactory, but downright delightful. Remember, the goal here isn't to be a creepy spy; it's about understanding your audience so well that you could practically finish their sentences.

But hang on, there's more! You can also gather insights through good old-fashioned conversations. Yes, I'm talking about that ancient art known as "talking to people." Engage with customers during interactions, whether it's in-store, at events, or even through good ol' customer support calls. Ask open-ended questions, and for goodness' sake, *listen*! You might be surprised at what customers will share when they feel like you genuinely care. They might spill the beans on what they love or, perhaps more importantly, what they don't love about your product. And while the latter might sting a little, it's better than being blindsided by a wave of negative reviews later.

Of course, the key to successful listening is not just about gathering information; it's about acting on it. This is where the magic truly happens! Take those customer insights and weave them into your business strategy. If customers are clamoring for a feature you didn't even know they wanted, it's time to roll up your sleeves and make it happen. Not only will this improve their experience, but it'll also show them that you're listening, not just passively, but actively. It's like serving them their favorite dessert after they've been hinting at it for weeks; you'll become the hero of their customer journey! That peanut butter ice cream…

Sorry, I'm back.

Lastly, don't underestimate the power of humor in your listening strategy. Sometimes, customers drop their guard when they sense a little levity in the conversation. Use witty surveys or playful social media posts to encourage feedback. You might just find that a sprinkle of humor can lead to more candid comments and a deeper connection.

To summarize, "eavesdrop" on your customers (legally, remember), create a listening culture within your organization, and turn those insights into action. Because in the end, crafting connections is all about making your customers feel heard, valued, and maybe even entertained along the way!

Chapter 3 | Designing a Beautiful Customer Experience Is the Blueprint for Success

Mapping the Customer Journey: It's Not Just a Sunday Drive

Mapping the customer journey may sound like a weekend drive, a leisurely jaunt where everything unfolds beautifully, and you can stop for ice cream whenever you want. In reality, it's more like navigating a maze while blindfolded, with unexpected detours, potholes, and that one infuriating GPS voice that keeps yelling "recalculating." In effect, it's a Japanese gameshow.

Business leaders and entrepreneurs must understand that the customer journey is not just a path to conversion; it's a complex expedition filled with twists, turns, and the occasional roadside attraction that might just lead to a delightful surprise. Or a flat tire.

First, let's face the fact that every customer experience is unique. While some may glide smoothly from awareness to purchase like a well-oiled machine, others may feel like they're caught in a never-ending loop of "Are we there yet?" It's essential to map this journey with precision, taking into account the various touchpoints where customers might pause, ponder, or completely freak out. Imagine a tourist trying to find the bathroom in a massive theme park. Are you really going to let your customers wander aimlessly through your brand without a map? Spoiler alert: They will likely end up in the competitor's restroom.

When crafting this customer journey map, humor can be a great companion. Think about it: if your customers are having fun, they're more likely to stick around. Instead of a dull, corporate-speak document filled with jargon, why not create a vibrant, engaging visual that captures the essence of their journey? Use playful illustrations, relatable scenarios, and maybe even a cartoon of a disgruntled customer battling a wild customer service robot. This approach not only makes the process enjoyable but also helps everyone in the organization understand the customer experience from a fresh perspective. Because wouldn't you want a good laugh while discussing customer pain points?

Measuring the success of this journey is akin to determining how much you've enjoyed that Sunday drive. I'm sure you've heard this one before: It's not just about the destination; it's about the memories you make along the way. Collecting metrics and analytics can feel like a tedious chore, but it's essential for understanding customer sentiment. Implement a few humorous metrics, like "number of ice cream stops" (representing delightful interactions) versus "detours to the wrong exit" (representing frustrating experiences). This light-hearted approach can help keep your team engaged and focused on improving the overall customer experience. Because, let's face it, no one enjoys being stuck in traffic, especially if it's caused by poor service.

Ultimately, mapping the customer journey is an ongoing adventure, not a one-time event. Just like your favorite road trip playlist, it needs constant updating to keep things fresh and exciting. Business leaders and corporate stakeholders should embrace this journey as a dynamic process, constantly refining their strategies based on customer feedback and evolving preferences.

Touchpoints Galore: Creating Moments That Matter (And Avoiding Awkward Silences)

You know how it is in the movie theatre; the popcorn can be wildly unpredictable: some pop, some flop, and the occasional rogue kernel may even hit you in the face. That's exactly how touchpoints are in Customer Experience. Understanding these touchpoints is crucial for creating memorable moments that resonate with customers.

Picture this: a customer walks into a store and is greeted by an enthusiastic employee who might as well be auditioning for a Broadway show. A good one though... Not all shows are created equal. This is a touchpoint that can make the difference between a delightful visit and a head-scratching "What just happened?" moment. The goal is to curate touchpoints that shine brighter than a disco ball at a '70s party (respect your elders), ensuring that every interaction is not just a moment but a memorable experience.

Now, let's talk about the dreaded awkward silence. You know the one – the conversation lags, and you can practically hear crickets chirping in the background. In the context of Customer Experience, these silences can be just as painful. Imagine a customer walking into a café only to be met with an employee who looks like they just woke up from a nap. The silence stretches out, and the customer is left pondering their life choices. To avoid these cringe-worthy moments, it's essential to equip your team with conversation starters and engaging questions. Think of it like training them to be the life of the party, but instead of karaoke, they're serving lattes and smiles.

Creating moments that matter is all about intention. Businesses can craft experiences that resonate by mapping out the customer journey like a treasure map leading to the ultimate prize: *customer satisfaction*. Each touchpoint should be a delightful surprise, like finding an extra fry at the bottom of the bag. This can include personalized emails, surprise discounts, a customer of the week board, or follow-up calls that don't sound like a robot reciting a script. By injecting a bit of personality into these interactions, businesses can transform routine exchanges into memorable experiences that have customers talking in a good way, instead of becoming fodder for their next social media rant.

Metrics and analytics are your best friends in this adventure. But let's be honest, the idea of poring over spreadsheets can feel as thrilling as watching paint dry. However, using data to understand touchpoints can help you avoid those awkward silences and create moments that matter. Analyzing customer feedback and behavior patterns is like having a crystal ball that reveals what your customers love, or what makes them cringe. By leveraging insights from surveys and engagement metrics, businesses can pivot and adapt their strategies, ensuring that each touchpoint is more delightful than the last, rather than a cringe-worthy misstep.

Finally, unless the context isn't right (like if you're a funeral service provider) I urge you once again to not be afraid to bring some humor into the mix. Humor can be a powerful tool in crafting connections. A well-timed joke or a light-hearted comment can break the ice and turn an ordinary touchpoint into a memorable interaction. Imagine a customer service representative who, rather than delivering the usual "How may I assist you?" comes in with, "I promise I'm more helpful than that tiny wiper they stuck on your rear windshield!" This approach not only diffuses tension but also fosters a friendly atmosphere that customers are likely to remember.

By embracing a humorous tone and being intentional about each interaction, businesses can create an experience that customers will not only enjoy but also share with others, effectively turning them into champions of your brand.

Building a Customer-Centric Culture: It's Like Herding Cats, But Worth It

Building a customer-centric culture is a lot like herding cats. Imagine trying to get a group of independent-minded felines to follow a single path, all while they chase laser dots, nap in sunbeams, and staunchly ignore your pleas. Similarly, instilling a customer-first mindset in an organization is no walk in the park. Employees, like cats, come with their own personalities, motivations, and, let's face it, distractions. They may be more inclined to chase their own goals than to focus on the customer experience. But fear not, it can be done! With the right approach, you can create a culture that puts customers at the forefront, even if it requires a bit of clever coaxing and a sprinkle of catnip.

First, you need to create an environment where everyone understands that the customer is the boss. This means crafting a vision statement that doesn't read like a legal contract but instead makes employees feel like they're joining a secret society dedicated to customer happiness. Think "Customer Experience Avengers" rather than "The Office of Customer Compliance." Encourage your team to think like customers themselves. Invite them to experience your products or services from a customer's perspective.

After all, nothing says "I understand your pain" like realizing that the "easy return policy" actually involves a scavenger hunt worthy of a treasure map.

Next, be prepared for some serious cat-and-mouse dynamics. Some team members will embrace the customer-centric culture with the enthusiasm of a kitten seeing a ball of yarn, while others might be more like the aloof feline that prefers to watch from afar. To tackle this, employ some creative tactics. Reward those who go above and beyond in their customer-impacting activities with fun incentives. Think "Customer Experience Champion" badges or even a goofy trophy that sits on their desk, reminding everyone that they are the real heroes of customer satisfaction. Who doesn't want to feel like a superstar in a world where everyone else is just trying to avoid the vacuum cleaner?

Communication is key, but let's be honest, not everyone reads the company newsletter with the same fervor as a cat watches birds outside the window. To keep everyone engaged, leverage humor in your messaging. Use funny anecdotes, memes, or even short videos that highlight the importance of Customer Experience. A viral cat video juxtaposed with a message about customer feedback could do wonders for engagement. Remember, people are more likely to remember a lesson when it's wrapped in a laugh. This approach not only keeps the momentum going but also makes the whole process feel less like a chore and more like a delightful romp through a field of catnip.

Finally, embrace the chaos. There will be a few scary missteps, misunderstandings, and moments that leave you scratching your head. Celebrate those moments as opportunities for growth. Encourage your team to share their "catastrophic" customer service stories in a light-hearted way, creating a safe space for learning. When employees feel supported and part of a team, they are more likely to embrace the customer-centric mindset.

Arm yourself with patience, sprinkle in a little humor, and get ready to laugh your way to a thriving customer-centric culture. After all, it's not just about herding cats; it's about creating a community of feline enthusiasts dedicated to making every customer experience *purr-fect.*

Chapter 4 | The Secret Sauce of Customer Engagement: It's Not Ketchup

Personalization, Because Nobody Wants to Feel Like a Number

Personalization in Customer Experience is a bit like a well-tailored suit; it makes you feel dapper, and, let's face it, a little more special. Nobody wants to walk into a store or browse a website and feel like just another face in the crowd. Imagine being greeted with "Hey, you! Yes, you! The one with the vaguely human shape!" instead of a warm welcome. Personalization is the antidote to that awkward moment when you realize you're just a number, like the unfortunate soul stuck at Table 13 during the family reunion, hoping for a miracle while everyone else is enjoying their own slice of pie.

In the world of Customer Experience, personalization is not just a trendy buzzword; it's a necessity. When businesses take the time to understand their customers' preferences, behaviors, and quirks, they can craft experiences that resonate on a personal level. Think of it as a matchmaking service, but instead of playing Cupid, companies connect customers with products and services they'll truly love. Nobody wants to be bombarded with irrelevant ads featuring products they'd never consider, like a dance class for people who can't find their left foot. Instead, they want recommendations that say, "Yo, we get you! You might like this because you have excellent taste."

The beauty of personalization lies in the data. Yes, data – the mysterious force that can feel as daunting as a calculus exam. I know. But by leveraging analytics, businesses can uncover valuable insights about their customers. It's like having a magic crystal ball that reveals what customers are thinking, minus the swirling smoke and questionable fortune teller. By analyzing past purchases and browsing habits, companies can predict future needs and even avoid the dreaded "I've seen that before" syndrome. After all, nothing says "I care" like showing up with the perfect gift instead of a random novelty item that screams "last-minute shopping."

Now, let's address the elephant in the room: the fine line between personalization and stalking. There's a difference between being attentive and being creepy. No one wants to feel like they're being followed around the internet like an evil clown. Businesses must tread carefully and respect customer privacy while still delivering those tailored experiences. A little humor can go a long way here; imagine a brand saying, "We see you browsing our shoes. We're not watching you, just admiring your impeccable taste from afar." It's all about striking the right balance between making customers feel special and not turning them into a case study in overreach.

Finally, let's not forget that personalization isn't a one-time event; it's an ongoing relationship. Like any good romance, it requires effort, attention, and sometimes a little bit of charm. Businesses should continuously engage with their customers, adapting to their evolving preferences and needs. Regular check-ins, personalized offers, and even a cheeky pun can keep the connection alive. Also, don't sleep on the effectiveness of letting the customers themselves tell you what they like, love or dislike. Those heart and thumbs up/down buttons are there on your streaming services for a reason,

Remember, personalization is the secret sauce that transforms the mundane into the magical. And at the end of the day, we're not asking for much; just to be treated like the VIPs we truly are.

Omnichannel Strategies: Meeting Customers Where They Are (Even in Their PJs)

Today, customers have more options than ever, and they expect businesses to be as accessible as their favorite pair of pajamas. An omnichannel strategy is like a well-thought-out playbook that fits every occasion, including those lazy Sunday mornings when your customers are still in their PJs, scrolling through their phones. Whether they're in a coffee shop, at home, or even sneaking a peek during a meeting, your business needs to be right there, ready to serve them.

No more waiting for customers to come to you; it's time to bring the experience to their couch!

Imagine your customer lounging at home, sipping coffee, and suddenly remembering they need a new blender. They pull out their phone, hop onto your website, and voila! They see that not only can they buy their perfect blender online, but they can also pick it up at the nearest store or have it delivered faster than a pizza. This seamless experience is what omnichannel strategies are all about. Just when they thought they were going to have to trudge out to the store in their fuzzy slippers, you make it easy for them to get what they need without compromising their comfort.

Now, let's talk about the importance of consistency across channels. Your customers are like a well-caffeinated squirrel on a sugar rush. They're bouncing from one platform to another, and they expect the same delightful experience no matter where they land. If they start browsing your products on Instagram while wearing their favorite PJs, they shouldn't feel like they've stepped into a parallel universe when they switch to your website. Keep your messaging, branding, and user experience aligned, so they know they're still dealing with the same friendly face, even if you're not physically there to hand them the shopping bag.

But don't forget about the power of data! Just like a good detective, you need to gather clues from various customer interactions to build a comprehensive picture of their preferences and behaviors. These insights allow you to anticipate their needs and offer personalized recommendations, like a long-time friend suggesting a movie you'll love because they know your taste in rom coms. With analytics at your disposal, you can tailor your offerings to meet customers where they are, whether it's in their PJs or dressed to the nines for a night out. Remember, every click, scroll, and purchase is a piece of the puzzle that helps you understand your customers better.

In conclusion, embracing omnichannel strategies is not just about being present on multiple platforms; it's about creating a cohesive and enjoyable customer experience that meets your audience in their moments of need, regardless of their attire. In a world where convenience reigns supreme, your ability to engage customers while they're lounging at home or dashing between meetings will set you apart from the competition. So, get ready to put on your best virtual face and show up for your customers, PJs or not! After all, who wouldn't want to be the business that makes shopping so easy, it feels like a cozy weekend morning?

The Power of Storytelling: How to Turn Customers into Raving Fans

Picture this: a customer walks into your store, glances at a product, and within five seconds decides to leave without even considering a purchase. What went wrong? Maybe your display was as exciting as watching paint dry. Now imagine if, instead, that customer was greeted with a captivating story about how that product saved a family from a zombie apocalypse. Suddenly, they're not just buying a blender; they're investing in a slice of an epic tale. This illustrates the magic of storytelling in transforming ordinary transactions into memorable experiences that can turn customers into raving fans.

When it comes to storytelling, it's not just about spinning yarns that would put your grandma to sleep. It's about crafting narratives that resonate with your audience. If you can weave a tale that connects with their emotions, be it joy, nostalgia, or the sheer thrill of adventure, you're not just selling a product; you're selling a whole experience. Think about the companies that do this well. They don't just sell shoes; they sell the dream of running a marathon while battling a fire-breathing dragon. And who wouldn't want to buy that kind of footwear?

Now, let's talk strategy. You might be thinking, "That all sounds great, but how do I actually implement storytelling in my customer experience?" Let's double-click! You don't need to hire a team of Shakespearean actors or build a Broadway set in your office. Start by identifying the core values of your business and the stories that stem from those values. Use anecdotes from your team or feedback from your customers to create relatable narratives. Remember, authenticity is key. If your story sounds like a corporate brochure, you'll lose your audience faster than you can say "customer churn."

Metrics, you say? Yes, even the most riveting stories need a bit of number crunching. You can't just throw a story out into the wild and hope it catches on like a viral cat video. Only cats have that power. Use analytics to gauge which stories resonate the most with your customers. Are they sharing your tales on social media? Are they more likely to purchase after hearing a particular story? By measuring the impact of your storytelling efforts, you can refine your approach, ensuring that your narratives hit home and ignite customer loyalty.

In the end, remember that every customer interaction is an opportunity to tell a story. Whether it's the moment they discover your product or the experience of using it, every touchpoint can be a chapter in their journey with your brand. By harnessing the power of storytelling, you can turn your customers into raving fans, which, let's be honest, is a lot more fun than simply being a 'repeat buyer.'

Chapter 5 | Metrics That Matter: Measuring Customer Experience Without Losing Your Mind

KPIs: Key Performance Indicators or Keeping People Irritated?

In business, KPIs typically stand for Key Performance Indicators, but let's be honest, they might just as well translate to Keeping People Irritated. Here's a picture for you: you're drowning in a sea of metrics, each one more convoluted than the last, while your team looks like they've just been asked to solve the mysteries of the universe. When your morning meetings start sounding like a game show where no one wants to win, it's time to reevaluate your approach to KPIs.

Let's break down the classic KPI dilemma. You have your Net Promoter Score, Customer Satisfaction Score, and Customer Effort Score. Sounds impressive, right? But if you're not careful, these metrics can become the equivalent of a toddler's tantrum: loud, dramatic, and entirely unhelpful. Sure, they're designed to give you insight into how your customers feel, but if you're not translating that data into action, you might as well be reading tea leaves. The last thing you want is to be that company that has a chart for everything but still manages to trip over its own shoelaces.

Consider the universal truth that not all metrics are created equal. Some KPIs are like that one friend who always shows up to the party uninvited and insists on telling the same bad joke. You know the ones – like tracking the number of customers who clicked on an email but didn't buy anything. Sure, it's a stat, but does it actually matter? Instead, focus on those indicators that actually illuminate the path forward, like customer retention rates or repeat purchase behavior. These are your VIPs in the KPI world, and they're the ones who can really help you craft a stellar customer experience.

Now, let's talk about the inevitable KPI fatigue that sets in when you throw too many metrics at your team. You know how it goes: one day everyone's enthusiastic, diligently tracking everything under the sun, and the next, they're staring blankly at a spreadsheet like it's a math problem from a bad dream. The solution? Keep it simple! Choose a handful of KPIs that align with your goals and make them fun. Instead of a boring old meeting to review metrics, how about a "KPI Cook-Off" where teams compete to come up with the most creative ways to boost those numbers? Bonus points for snacks!

Ultimately, the goal of KPIs should be to foster collaboration and innovation, not to induce eye rolls and sighs of frustration. When business leaders remember that the purpose of these indicators is to enhance the customer experience, they can turn the tide from irritation to inspiration. So, the next time you're tempted to drown your team in a deluge of metrics, remember: KPIs should be tools for growth, not just another reason for people to shake their heads and mutter under their breath. After all, if your KPIs aren't making your customer experience better, they might just be keeping people irritated. And nobody wants that.

NPS, CSAT, and Other Acronyms: Decoding the Customer Experience Language

To the casual outsider, CX acronyms are the secret handshake that separates the initiated few from the rest of the civilian population. You might have heard of NPS, CSAT, and a few others that sound like the latest tech gadgets. But don't worry, we're not here to make you feel like you've walked into a meeting held entirely in Klingon (unless you're actually from Qo'noS). Instead, we'll decode these terms together, with a sprinkle of humor to keep you awake and engaged, because who doesn't love a good laugh while learning?

Let's kick things off with NPS, or Net Promoter Score, which sounds fancy but is really just a way to gauge how likely your customers are to recommend your business to their friends. Imagine that your customers are at a party, and they're asked whether they would shout your name from the rooftops or hide in a corner when someone mentions your brand. The NPS is the difference between the roof-shouters (promoters) and the party poopers (detractors). It's like a high school popularity contest, but instead of being voted "Most Likely to Succeed," you want to avoid being "Most Likely to End Up in the Spam Folder."

Now, let's talk about CSAT, or Customer Satisfaction Score. This is like the baby brother of NPS, always trying to earn his stripes. CSAT is basically the "How'd we do?" question right after a customer interacts with your company. Picture a waiter asking if your meal was delicious while you're still chewing. A little awkward, right? The goal is to get feedback before customers can change their minds, and it's often expressed as a percentage. So if 80% of your customers are satisfied, congratulations! You're not just surviving; you're thriving. Unless, of course, that 20% is planning a social media smear campaign.

There are a bunch more acronyms, but let's just take a look at CES (Customer Effort Score), which measures how easy it is for customers to interact with your service. Think of it as the "How Many Clicks Does It Take to Get to the Center of Your Service?" challenge. Customers are busy people, and if they're spending more time navigating your website than they would on a Netflix binge, you might want to rethink your design strategy. The goal is to make it so easy that even a confused octopus could find what they need without ripping their tentacles out in frustration.

In the end, these acronyms are more than just letters strung together; they're your roadmap to understanding the customer journey. By keeping an eye on NPS, CSAT, CES, and a few others, you'll be well on your way to crafting a customer experience that makes people rave about your brand instead of roll their eyes. Bear in mind that with Customer Experience, the only thing worse than a confusing acronym is a confusing experience. It's okay for you and your team to keep a leather-bound glossary book handy to decode all the acronyms, but as soon as you start confusing the customer, you might as well throw the book, and your entire business projection, into the trash.

The Feedback Loop: How to Ask for Feedback Without Sounding Desperate

Asking for feedback can feel a bit like asking someone to judge your art project from kindergarten. You dread the thought of them pulling out a red marker and writing "Needs Improvement" across your carefully constructed masterpiece. But I've got some good news for you: there's a way to solicit feedback without sounding like you're desperately fishing for compliments or, worse, begging for validation. The key lies in the approach you take, and a bit of tasteful humor can go a long way in transforming that dreaded moment into a delightful exchange.

First, let's tackle the elephant in the room: the fear of looking needy. Nobody wants to be the person at the party who keeps asking, "Do you like my outfit? How about now?

What if I add this hat?" Instead, consider framing your request for feedback as a casual chat over coffee. Preferably a fancy coffee with a name that sounds like it belongs in a yoga studio. You might say, "Hey, I'm trying to improve your experience with me. What do you think? Your insights would be like sprinkles on a cupcake – delicious and 100% necessary!" This way, you invite input while keeping the vibe light and fun.

Next, remember that humor can be your best friend. Instead of sending a bland email that reads like a legal document, try adding a dash of personality. Imagine your colleague opening an email that says, "I'm seeking your feedback because I trust your taste more than I trust my Netflix recommendations. Seriously, if you have any thoughts on my latest project, let's hear them." This not only warms up the conversation but also shows that you're human and approachable. After all, who doesn't enjoy a good chuckle while contributing to your success?

When you're requesting feedback, specificity is key. You wouldn't ask someone how they feel about your cooking without specifying whether you want to know about the toast or the pasta. Instead of a vague "What do you think?" try something like, "I'm looking for feedback on our latest interaction, specifically, how easy it was for you to find what you needed. I'm on a quest to make sure the vibes stay immaculate!" This lets your audience know exactly what you're after, making them more likely to lend their insights without feeling overwhelmed by the task.

Lastly, don't forget to follow up with gratitude and a touch of humor, even if the feedback is brutally honest. A simple "Thanks for your feedback! Not all heroes wear capes." can make sure the exercise ends on a positive note. Acknowledging the input not only shows appreciation but also invites future conversations. Your parents were right after all when they taught you the importance of saying "please" and "thank you"!

Chapter 6 | The Future of CX: Trends That Will Make You Go "Hmmm"

AI and Automation: Your New Customer Service Coworkers

So, check this out: You're sitting at your desk, ready to tackle the day, when suddenly your computer chimes in with a friendly greeting, "Good morning! I'm here to help you solve customer queries faster than you can say 'the singularity!'" That's right, folks! Welcome to the era of AI and automation, where your new customer service coworkers are not only highly efficient but also have zero need for coffee breaks or HR complaints. If you ever wanted a team member who never sleeps, never eats, and never complains about being overworked, congratulations! You'll love it here.

Now, before you start imagining your corporate office filling up with robot assistants in neon suits, let's talk about how these AI systems actually work. They're like the super-smart interns who have read every customer service manual ever written, memorized all the FAQs, and can churn out responses in milliseconds. They're programmed to learn from past interactions, so the more they work, the better they get, kind of like that one colleague who keeps getting promotions while you're still trying to figure out the coffee machine. With AI handling the repetitive tasks, your human team can focus on the more complex and emotional aspects of customer service. Yes, I'm talking about the art of soothing a distressed customer who just found out their favorite product is out of stock.

But let's not overlook the potential hiccups along the way. Imagine an AI trying to crack a joke while troubleshooting a customer's issue, only to respond with, "Why did the customer cross the road? To get to the other side of the complaint!" Facepalm. While AI can analyze data and predict trends, it doesn't quite grasp the nuances of human emotion. This is where your human touch comes in. It's essential to strike a balance between automation and personal interaction, ensuring customers feel valued and understood. I think we can all agree that no one wants to feel like they're chatting with a glorified calculator.

Now, integrating AI and automation into your customer experience strategy shouldn't be about replacing humans; it's about enhancing your service. Think of AI as your trusty sidekick, handling the grunt work and leaving you free to swoop in and save the day when things get tricky. By leveraging customer experience metrics and analytics provided by these systems, you can gain insights into customer behavior, preferences, and pain points. It's like having a crystal ball that tells you what your customers want even before they're fully conscious about wanting it. Just remember, with great power comes great responsibility, young Petey. Use these insights wisely, or you might end up suggesting a dog biscuit product to a dedicated cat-dad.

In conclusion, embracing AI and automation in CX is not merely about jumping on the tech bandwagon; it's about crafting connections that stick. As business leaders and professionals, you have the opportunity to redefine the Customer Experience landscape, blending the efficiency of AI with the empathy of human interaction. So, gear up to welcome your new AI colleagues and prepare for a future where Customer Experience is not just a department but a delightful journey. And who knows? Your AI might even help you win that "Best Customer Experience" award, and that's fine, just as long as you don't let it give the acceptance speech.

The Rise of the Experience Economy: When Experiences Are Worth More Than Stuff

We've all seen the curtain rise on the Experience Economy, where a thrilling roller coaster ride or a blissful spa day can outshine a shiny new gadget. Yes folks, we've officially reached the point where people would rather spend their hard-earned cash on an Instagram-worthy brunch than on a new set of kitchen knives. Who knew that avocado toast made a specific way by a specific chef at a specific restaurant could become a status symbol? As consumers increasingly prioritize experiences over possessions, businesses must adapt faster than a barista eagerly spelling your name wrong on a coffee cup.

Imagine walking into a store where instead of being bombarded with products, you're greeted by a friendly llama (or a similar quirky mascot). Suddenly, you're not just there to buy; you're there to experience, perhaps to pet the llama, take a selfie, and post it to social media, complete with the hashtag #LlamaLove and #ILove[insert name of the business]. In this new economy, it's all about creating memorable moments that customers will rave about to their friends and family. The key lies in crafting these experiences so that customers walk away feeling like they've just participated in meaningful, heartwarming experience, rather than simply completed a mundane transaction.

For business leaders and entrepreneurs, this shift means rethinking how we deliver value. It's not enough to just sell a product; we have to sell a story, an experience, or a journey. Think about it: how many times have you purchased a product because of the compelling narrative behind it? When consumers feel emotionally connected, they'll choose your brand over a competitor's, even if that competitor has the latest tech gadget that promises to chop, dice, and julienne in a single bound. You can't tell iPhone users nothing! If you can create an experience that resonates, you'll have customers returning faster than you can say "customer loyalty."

Metrics and analytics, the unsung heroes of the corporate world, need a makeover too. Instead of just tracking sales figures and conversion rates, don't be afraid to get a little creative. Start measuring the joy factor. How many smiles did your experience generate? How many social media shares did that llama photo receive? By incorporating these more whimsical metrics, you can gain insight into what truly resonates with your audience, guiding your strategy and helping you craft even better experiences in the future. Understand that if you can quantify the magic, you can replicate it!

As we dive deeper into this Experience Economy, remember that it's not just about giving customers what they want; it's about surprising them with what they didn't know they needed. So, dust off those creative thinking caps and get ready to revolutionize your approach. Because, let's face it, nobody is going to brag about their new blender at a dinner party. But if you can offer them an experience that leaves them laughing, sharing stories, and perhaps even craving a bit more llama love, you'll have truly won their hearts and minds. And isn't that what we all want?

Sustainability: Why Your Customers Want You to Save the Planet (And How to Do It)

Sustainability, like Customer Experience, isn't just a trendy buzzword to toss around at your next corporate retreat while sipping organic green smoothies. Nowadays, customers are more environmentally conscious than ever, and they want to know that the companies they support aren't just in it for the profit but are also trying to save the planet that we all literally need to exist. Think of your customers as eco-warriors in disguise, dressed in yoga pants and armed with reusable shopping bags, they're ready to scrutinize every aspect of your business from your packaging to your carbon footprint. So, if you want to win their hearts (and wallets), it's time to embrace sustainability like a warm, fuzzy blanket made from recycled materials.

You might be wondering how to make your business more sustainable without sacrificing your bottom line, or your sanity. The road to sustainability is paved with opportunities that can actually enhance your Customer Experience. Start by examining your supply chain. Are you sourcing materials from companies that practice sustainable methods, or are you still using suppliers from a bygone era when coal was the cleanest energy source?

Customers love transparency, so don't be afraid to share your eco-friendly sourcing stories. Picture it: your marketing campaign could feature a heartwarming video of you walking through the woods while explaining how you're planting a tree for every product sold. Customers will eat it up; figuratively, of course, unless you're selling edible trees. The important thing here is to not make these stories up or exaggerate them. Actually do the thing you say you're doing, because if you don't, your customers will eventually find out. And when they do, the fallout will be so bad, you'll wish you'd never heard the word, "sustainability" to begin with.

Let's not forget about the packaging... oh, the packaging! If your boxes are bigger than the items inside, your customers might start to wonder if you're secretly running a side gig as a magician. This used to be a running joke in my household, when a certain company (let's call it *Nozama*) would routinely deliver a phone charger in a box large enough to contain the phone charger factory. In recent years though, they seem to be paying more attention to this, so, good for them! Opt for minimal, eco-friendly packaging solutions that make your products feel like precious treasures instead of landfills in waiting.

Plus, who doesn't love unboxing a product that's wrapped in recycled newsprint and adorned with biodegradable confetti? It's the kind of delightful surprise that makes customers want to share your brand on social media, and we all know that free marketing is like finding a $20 bill in your winter coat pocket.

Now, let's talk metrics (again) because what's a good strategy without some numbers to back it up? Start tracking your sustainability efforts and share those metrics with your customers. Did you reduce your waste by 30% last year? Fantastic! That's a reason to throw a party, or at least a social media post that's more exciting than yet another cat video. By showcasing your progress, you'll not only build trust but also inspire your customers to join you on this eco-journey. After all, no one wants to be the only one eating kale at a barbecue.

In conclusion, making sustainability a core part of your business strategy isn't just good for the planet; it's also a fantastic way to enhance your Customer Experience. By aligning your values with those of your customers, you're not just selling products; you're building a community of like-minded individuals who care about the Earth as much as they care about their favorite avocado toast. So, embrace sustainability with open arms and watch as your customer loyalty blossoms. When your customers see that you care about saving the planet, they'll be more inclined to invest in your brand, one eco-friendly product at a time.

Chapter 7 | Crafting Connections: Real-Life CX Stories Worth Your Attention

Brands That Nailed It: CX Wins You'll Want to Copy

When it comes to Customer Experience, some brands have mastered the art like a seasoned chef whipping up their signature meal. Take Zappos, for instance. Their customer service is legendary, and not just because they once sent a customer a pizza when their order was delayed. Zappos encourages employees to go above and beyond, which means if you're ever feeling down, you might just get a friendly call from a rep who will cheer you up with a heartfelt conversation, and maybe a joke or two. If you want to replicate this success, remember: it's not just about selling shoes; it's about building a community one quirky interaction at a time.

Then there's Netflix, the streaming service that knows how to keep customers glued to their screens like a toddler to a candy store. They've taken personalization to an alarming level, recommending shows based on your viewing history with the precision of a psychic at a carnival. Who knew that watching a documentary about the history of cheese would lead you to a romantic drama? Their use of data analytics to tailor content keeps subscribers entertained and coming back for more, while also making it seem like they know you better than your own family. So, if you're looking to enhance your customer experience, consider how data can help you predict what your customers want before they even know it themselves.

Let's not forget about Starbucks, the caffeine giant that has turned ordering coffee into an experience worthy of an art exhibition. With their mobile app, customers can order ahead and skip the line, making it feel like they have a VIP pass to the coffee world. Not to mention, their baristas are trained to remember names and customize orders to the nth degree. Who wouldn't want their daily caffeine fix prepared just the way they like it, by someone who knows their name and has probably memorized their life story? If you want to nail the customer experience, take a page out of Starbucks' playbook: make every interaction feel personal and allow customers to feel like they're not just another number in the system.

Then there's Amazon, the ultimate one-stop-shop where you can buy everything from a book on how to juggle to a life-sized inflatable dinosaur. Their customer experience is so seamless that it feels like magic. One click and your item is on its way to your doorstep faster than you can say "two-day shipping." Their return policy is so generous that you might think they want to become your new best friend. By prioritizing convenience and accessibility, Amazon has transformed shopping into a delightful experience. So, if you want to keep your customers coming back, consider how you can streamline their journey and make them feel like they've hit the jackpot with every purchase.

Finally, let's talk about Disney, "the happiest place on Earth", where even the lines for rides feel like part of the experience. With their *My Disney Experience* app, guests can book FastPasses and plan their day like a military operation, because what's more magical than avoiding long queues? Disney's attention to detail is unmatched, from the cleanliness of the parks to the friendly cast members who treat you like royalty. They've nailed the customer experience by ensuring that every moment is filled with a sprinkle of magic and a dash of nostalgia. If you want to create CX that leaves people raving, take a page from Disney: make every interaction memorable and sprinkle in some joy along the way.

Lessons from the Trenches: What Not to Do

Because I believe that people (and in this case, companies) should not be reduced to their biggest embarrassing mistakes, I have intentionally left out names. But these stories are so well known, you may recognize them anyway. That said, this personal policy only applies to companies that have unwittingly embarrassed themselves. I have absolutely no problem spelling out the full name and mailing address of companies that have intentionally or carelessly brought true harm to customers, employees and communities.

In the wild world of Customer Experience, there are potholes aplenty, and navigating around them is essential if you want to avoid a spectacular faceplant. One of the most famous missteps comes from a well-meaning airline that decided to launch a new customer loyalty program. Unfortunately, they forgot to consult their customers first. The result: a rewards system so complicated that it could only be deciphered by a team of cryptographers. Customers were left scratching their heads, wondering if they'd accidentally signed up for a secret society instead of earning free flights. Lesson number one: always test your ideas on actual customers before unleashing them upon the world. Otherwise, you might end up with a loyalty program that's more confusing than a Rubik's cube at a toddler's birthday party.

Next on our list of "what not to do" is the infamous case of the fast-food chain that thought it would be a great idea to make their drive-thru experience more "efficient" by eliminating the human touch. Instead of cheerful employees taking orders, customers were greeted by an automated voice that sounded like it had just come from a 1980s sci-fi movie. The result? Order accuracy plummeted faster than a lead balloon, and customers were left wondering if they'd ordered fries with their burger, or a side of existential crisis. When it comes to Customer Experience, remember that people appreciate a human connection, even if it's just a friendly "Welcome to our restaurant!" from someone who doesn't sound like a malfunctioning robot.

Let's not forget the tech giant that rolled out a new app to enhance customer interaction, only to inadvertently turn their user base into a bunch of frustrated tech support agents. The app crashed more often than a clumsy toddler on roller skates, and customers spent more time troubleshooting than actually enjoying the services. Instead of a seamless experience, users found themselves in an endless loop of "Have you tried turning it off and on again?" This scenario highlights the importance of thorough testing and robust customer support. Launching new tech without ensuring it's user-friendly is like serving a gourmet meal without checking if anyone has food allergies; it's bound to end badly.

Then there's the infamous retail store that decided to revamp its customer service training by introducing a new script that employees had to follow religiously. What happened? A team of robots who could recite the company mantra but couldn't engage in a genuine conversation to save their lives. Customers felt like they were talking to a wall rather than receiving assistance. This scenario serves as a reminder that while consistency is important, authenticity is king. Customers can tell when someone is reading from a script, and they appreciate a little personality with their service. In short, train your employees, but don't turn them into automated drones.

And lastly, we have the classic tale of the company that launched a social media campaign to connect with customers. However, they forgot one crucial element: monitoring the comments. When customers took to the internet to air their grievances, the company was too busy patting themselves on the back to notice. The result? A PR disaster that could have been avoided with a simple click.

Proactive engagement on social media is essential; ignoring customer feedback is like throwing a party and not inviting anyone, except for crickets. You get a chorus of angry tweets. So, if you're looking to craft connections rather than burn bridges, keep an eye on your online presence and be ready to engage.

The Customer Experience Revolution: Join or Get Left Behind

The Customer Experience Revolution isn't just a catchy phrase, it's the battle cry of every business that's tired of hearing crickets instead of cash registers ringing. Imagine a customer walks into your store, looks around, and promptly walks out, leaving behind only a faint echo of disappointment. It's as if they stepped into a time machine and landed in the 1980s, where customer service was a vague concept and "self-checkout" was just a fantasy. If you want to avoid becoming the punchline of a bad joke, it's time to embrace the revolution or risk being left behind like that last slice of fruitcake at an office party.

In this day and age, customers expect more than just a transaction; they want an experience that's as delightful as finding a small box of complementary cajun fries included in your delivery order. Gone are the days when businesses could simply put out a sign that says "Open" and call it a day. Even springing for the neon version doesn't quite cut it anymore. Today's consumers are savvy, and they have an attention span that quickly unsubscribes from products, services or content that don't almost instantly meet their needs and capture their imagination. To keep them engaged, you need to craft experiences that are not only memorable but also personalized. Remember, customers are not just buying a product; they're investing in a story, and you want to be the one telling it, preferably with a few laughs along the way.

Let's take a moment to talk about Customer Experience design and strategy. Think of it as throwing a party. If the music is off-key, the snacks are stale, and the vibe is more funeral than fiesta, you can bet your bottom dollar that guests will make a beeline for the door. A successful CX strategy is like the ultimate playlist: it needs to be carefully curated, full of your audience's favorite hits, and capable of keeping the energy up. It's about knowing when to drop the bass and when to slow it down for those heartfelt moments. If you don't have a strategy, you might as well be playing the kazoo at a rock concert. Nobody's going to stick around for that!

Now, let's not forget the importance of metrics and analytics in this grand adventure. It's not enough to assume your customers are happy; you need hard evidence, or you might as well be throwing darts in the dark. Tracking CX metrics is like having a GPS for your business journey. It tells you when you're veering off course, when you're cruising smoothly, and when it's time to hit the brakes before you crash and burn. By analyzing data, you can uncover the hidden gems of customer feedback that will guide you toward creating better experiences, rather than leaving you in the dark like a clueless driver without a map.

In conclusion, the Customer Experience Revolution is not just a trend; it's a survival tactic. Embrace it, or risk becoming the business equivalent of that outdated flip phone that no one wants anymore (although, those do seem to be making a comeback... but you get the point). The choice is yours: join the revolution, innovate, and create experiences that dazzle your customers, or get left behind, reminiscing about the good old days when a "thank you" was considered top-notch service. Remember, in this game, it's all about connection. Get out there, make some noise, and turn your customers into raving fans who can't help but share their stories.

Chapter 8 | Putting It All Together: Your Action Plan for CX Success

Developing a Customer Experience Strategy: Your Roadmap to Greatness

Developing a Customer Experience strategy is like planning a road trip, but instead of packing snacks and arguing about the playlist, you're gearing up to create delightful interactions that leave your customers saying, "Wow, that was awesome!" The first step on this journey is to map out your destination. This means defining what a great customer experience looks like for your business. Are you aiming for the luxurious resort experience or the charming roadside diner vibe? Once you've chosen your ambiance, you can start charting the course with clear objectives. Remember, without a GPS (or at least a good old-fashioned map), you might end up in the middle of nowhere with a flat tire and a cranky customer.

Next, you'll want to gather your crew, because no road trip is complete without a trusty team. This team should include people from all corners of your organization: marketing, sales, customer service, and even that one person in accounting who always has the best snacks. Each member should bring their unique perspective on customer impact and interactions. Encourage brainstorming sessions that feel more like a game show than a board meeting. The more ideas, the better! Just be sure to keep the brainstorming focused; otherwise, you might end up with a plan to launch a cat café instead of improving your Customer Experience.

Once your team has a list of ideas that could rival a buffet, it's time to prioritize. This is where the magic happens. Evaluate which changes will have the most impact on your Customer Experience and which ones can be executed without needing a corporate bailout. Use customer feedback and data metrics like a crystal ball to determine what your customers actually want. Remember, just because a feature sounds like a great idea doesn't mean your customers will appreciate it as much as you do. Think of it like offering broccoli to kids; just because it's healthy doesn't mean anyone is going to enjoy it.

Now that you've prioritized your ideas and selected the crème de la crème of enhancements, it's time to implement your strategy. Roll out these changes like a new product launch, complete with fanfare, confetti, and perhaps some quirky dance moves. Communicate clearly with your team about their roles in this execution phase and provide them with the necessary tools and training to ensure they don't feel like deer in headlights when a customer walks through the door. Remember, a well-prepared team can make the experience feel seamless, even if the reality is a bit more chaotic behind the curtain.

Finally, the road doesn't end here; it's just the beginning of a continuous journey. Just like a road trip requires regular pit stops for gas (or charge) and snacks, your Customer Experience strategy needs ongoing evaluation and refinement. Collect feedback, analyze data, and adjust your course as necessary. If a particular experience is falling flat, don't be afraid to pivot. The best road trips often lead to unexpected destinations, so embrace the detours and learn from them. After all, in the world of CX, the goal isn't just satisfaction; it's creating memorable moments that keep customers coming back, maybe even singing karaoke in the backseat!

Building a Customer Experience Team: Assembling Your Avengers

Every great story needs a compelling cast of characters, and your Customer Experience team is no different. Think of it as assembling a superhero squad, but instead of capes, they wear badges that say "Customer Champion." The first step in building this dream team is to identify the unique roles that will help you create magical moments for your customers. You'll need your Empathizers, the ones who can feel your customers' pain as if it were their own, and your Data Nerds, who can turn numbers into narratives faster than you can say "customer journey mapping."

Now, let's talk about the *Empathizer Extraordinaire*. This individual should have the emotional range of a seasoned actor and the listening skills of a therapist. They thrive on understanding customer emotions and can turn even the grumpiest of customers into lifelong fans with a warm smile and a heartfelt "I understand." They're the ones who remind the team that behind every statistic is a real person; probably with a cat named Mr. Whiskers, who is not happy about their latest order mix-up.

Next up, we have the *Data Whisperer*. This character is the wizard of analytics, capable of deciphering charts and graphs like they're reading a bedtime story. Their superpower lies in transforming raw data into actionable insights, giving the team a roadmap for improvement. They'll make sure that your CX strategies are not just based on gut feelings but on solid evidence. With their help, you'll no longer be throwing spaghetti at the wall to see what sticks; instead, you'll have a scientifically-backed menu of strategies that are bound to delight your customers.

Let's not forget the *Creative Maverick*. This is the team member who sees the world through a kaleidoscope and isn't afraid to shake things up. They're the ones who come up with quirky ideas that have the potential to become your brand's signature moves. Whether it's a surprise thank-you note that gets delivered by a dancing delivery person or an interactive online experience that makes customers feel like they're part of a movie, this character ensures your brand remains memorable. After all, who doesn't want to be the company that turns mundane transactions into unforgettable adventures?

Finally, every effective Customer Experience team needs a *Strategic Sage*. This person is the wise old owl of your operation, guiding the team with their extensive knowledge of Customer Experience best practices and industry trends. Their job is to keep everyone focused on the bigger picture while ensuring that the team doesn't get lost in the minutiae. They're the ones who remind you that while it's vital to celebrate small wins, you must also keep an eye on the ultimate goal: creating a seamless, delightful experience for every customer. With this ensemble cast in place, your Customer Experience team will be well-equipped to craft connections that resonate, inspire loyalty, and, ultimately, tell a story worth sharing.

Continuous Improvement: Because Perfection is Just a Myth (But We Can Try)

CX Perfection is like that elusive unicorn everyone talks about but few actually see. You know the one – perfectly designed processes, flawless customer interactions, and a team that never misses a beat. Sure, it sounds great, but let's face it: perfection is as real as a three-headed dragon. Instead of chasing this mythical beast, let's embrace the reality that improvement is a journey filled with missteps, bloopers, and occasional bursts of brilliance. After all, if we were perfect, we'd probably be boring, and nobody wants to be that.

Imagine your Customer Experience strategy as a never-ending buffet. You can pile your plate high with the latest trends, technologies, and metrics, but there's always room for more. Just when you think you've found the perfect combination of ingredients, a new dish comes along that catches your eye. But here's the kicker – it's not about stuffing yourself silly with every new idea; it's about sampling, tasting, and refining your approach. Some flavors will delight your customers, while others might make them cringe. The goal is to keep tasting and adjusting until you find the winning recipe.

One of the best things about continuous improvement is that it encourages a culture where failure is not just accepted but celebrated. Picture your team brainstorming over a whiteboard, tossing out ideas like confetti at a New Year's party. Some of those ideas will be brilliant; others will flop harder than a poorly executed high-five. But instead of hiding those failures under the rug, why not display them proudly? Every misstep is a stepping stone toward understanding your customers better and creating experiences that resonate. Plus, who doesn't love a good story about how you once tried to implement a chatbot that could only respond with meme references?

Metrics and analytics are your trusty sidekicks in this quest for improvement. They're like the friend who always knows where the best tacos are. But instead of just taking their word for it, you want to dig deeper and find out why those tacos are so great. Are they spicy? Are they served with a side of guacamole? In the same way, you should analyze your Customer Experience data to uncover insights that lead to actionable changes. Metrics can guide you in determining what's working and what's not, turning your chaotic journey into a well-planned adventure.

Ultimately, continuous improvement is about embracing the chaos and finding joy in the process. It's about taking a step back, laughing at your misadventures, and appreciating the small victories along the way. Each tweak and adjustment brings you closer to creating a Customer Experience that not only meets expectations but occasionally blows them out of the water. So, while perfection may remain a distant dream, the art of continuous improvement is a delightful reality, full of opportunities to connect with your customers in ways that make them feel valued and understood. And who knows? You might just find that chasing that elusive unicorn makes the ride all the more enjoyable.

Chapter 9 | Rolling with the Punches: The Art of Staying Relevant

The Importance of Adaptability: Change is the Only Constant (And In-Laws... Change and In-Laws)

In business, adaptability is the tightrope walker, balancing precariously between the ever-changing demands of customers and the relentless march of technology. Companies that cling to outdated strategies are like that uncle who refuses to upgrade his flip phone; they risk being left in the dust while competitors leap ahead with nimble, innovative approaches. Embracing change isn't just a nice-to-have in Customer Experience, it's a survival skill akin to knowing how to avoid the awkward questions at family dinners with your in-laws.

Let's paint the scene: you've just launched a shiny new product, and the marketing team is ready to celebrate. But wait! The market shifts, and suddenly your customers are more interested in eco-friendly options than the latest tech gadget. It's a classic case of "what just happened?" Adaptability allows businesses to pivot quickly, reassess their strategies, and cater to shifting consumer preferences without losing their minds, or their market share. It's about reading the room, and in business, that room is often filled with a bunch of unpredictable characters who change their minds faster than a toddler at dinner time.

Now, let's talk about metrics (yet again). In the realm of Customer Experience, metrics are like your in-laws' old photo albums – full of information, somewhat nostalgic, but can also be a bit overwhelming. However, understanding and analyzing these metrics is essential for adapting to change. By keeping an eye on customer feedback, behavior trends, and engagement levels, businesses can identify when to pivot and when to double down. Think of it as having a crystal ball, but instead of predicting the future, you're simply trying to avoid the disaster of launching a product no one wants. Agile businesses utilize this data to stay ahead of the curve, responding to customer needs with the speed of a well-prepared host anticipating all game preferences and dodging awkward dinner conversations.

The art of adaptability also lies in fostering a culture of openness and experimentation within teams. It's about encouraging employees to share their wild ideas, even if they sound as crazy as a cat in a dog park. When teams feel free to innovate and test new concepts, they can uncover Customer Experience solutions that might just become the next big thing. This culture of flexibility not only boosts morale but also drives creativity, which is essential in a landscape where customer expectations are soaring higher than your father-in-law's golf score. For the uninitiated, the objective is to keep it as low as possible... hole-in-one and all that.

Ultimately, adaptability is the secret sauce that keeps businesses relevant and thriving in a world where change is the only constant, except, of course, for your in-laws, who will never be convinced that wearing socks with sandals is not a timeless style. Embracing change requires a mindset that not only accepts but anticipates the unexpected. By prioritizing adaptability, businesses can forge deeper connections with customers, foster loyalty, and create experiences that are not only memorable but also adaptable to the whims of a fast-paced market. So, let's raise a toast to adaptability, the unsung hero of Customer Experience, helping businesses navigate the tumultuous waters of change, one awkward family dinner at a time.

Celebrating Your Wins: Because Who Doesn't Love a Good Party?

Celebrating your wins is like adding sprinkles to an already delicious cupcake; it makes the experience just that much sweeter. In the fast-paced world of business, where deadlines loom larger than life and customer expectations can feel like climbing Everest, it's easy to forget to stop and smell the roses, or in this case, pop the confetti. Whether it's landing a major client, rolling out a successful Customer Experience strategy, or simply surviving a Monday with your sanity intact, there's always a reason to throw a party. After all, who doesn't love a good excuse to eat cake and dance like nobody's watching?

Now, let's talk about the types of celebrations that can really jazz up your workplace. You could go the traditional route and host a formal dinner, where everyone pretends to enjoy dry chicken while secretly plotting their escape to the nearest taco truck. Or you could embrace your inner child and throw a full-blown carnival, complete with cotton candy, games, and maybe even a dunk tank for that one colleague who always microwaves fish in the office kitchen. The goal is to create an environment where everyone feels appreciated and excited, because nothing says "team spirit" like a pie-in-the-face contest.

Of course, it's not just about the fun and games; there's a method to this madness. Celebrating wins reinforces a culture of recognition and appreciation, which is essential for maintaining high morale and productivity. When employees feel valued, they're more likely to go the extra mile for customers, turning mundane interactions into memorable experiences. So, while you're tossing confetti, remember that you're also sowing the seeds of loyalty and engagement. It's like a two-for-one deal: a party for your team and a boost in customer experience.

Metrics are your best friends when it comes to celebrating wins. Track your achievements, no matter how small, and use them as fuel for your next shindig. Did your customer satisfaction score go up by a single percentage point? Break out the balloons! Did your social media engagement double? Time for a confetti shower! Celebrating these metrics not only highlights progress but also keeps the momentum going. You can even create a "Wall of Fame" in the office, where photos and stories of these victories are displayed like trophies. Just think of it as an Instagram feed for your workplace, minus the filters and hashtags.

In the end, celebrating your wins is about more than just a good time; it's about creating connections and building a culture that values success at every level. So, gather your team, crank up the music, and let loose! Whether it's a simple shout-out in a meeting or a lavish celebration, make sure your wins are acknowledged. Remember, a happy team translates to happy customers, and who doesn't want to ride that wave of positivity? After all, if you're managing to put together a grand symphony of excellent and improving Customer Experience, every win deserves a round of applause, preferably with a side of cake.

Staying Curious: The Key to Long-Term Success (And Lifelong Learning)

Staying curious is like being a cat with nine lives – each curiosity leads you down a new path, and you just might discover something amazing before you get distracted by a shiny object. As business leaders and entrepreneurs, it's crucial to embrace that childlike wonder. Remember when you were a kid, and every question was a chance to explore? Somewhere along the way, many of us traded that inquisitive spirit for spreadsheets and PowerPoints. But let's be real: if you want to stay ahead in Customer Experience, you need to channel your inner five-year-old. Instead of "Why is the sky blue?" it might be "Why do our customers prefer our competitors' offerings?" Spoiler alert: the answers could lead to groundbreaking insights.

Curiosity isn't just a feel-good buzzword; it's the secret sauce for innovation. There you are, sitting in a meeting, and someone mentions a new trend in Customer Experience. Instead of nodding along like a bobblehead, take a moment to ask questions. "What if we tried this?" or "How could we apply this to our business?" can turn a dull discussion into a brainstorming bonanza. When you approach challenges with curiosity, you open doors to ideas that might seem outlandish at first. Remember, every great idea started with someone daring to ask, "What if?" So, grab your metaphorical detective hat and start investigating everything, especially the feedback from your customers. They are the treasure map to your next big breakthrough

Now, let's talk about lifelong learning. The world of Customer Experience is changing faster than a toddler finding the highest possible human vocal pitch for their screams in the center of the grocery store when you say no to a third candy. If you're not keeping up, you might find yourself left behind, like that one person still clipping a pager to their hip. The best part? Learning doesn't have to feel like a chore. It can be as enjoyable as binge-watching your favorite series. Except, instead of cliffhangers, you'll have insights waiting for you at the end of each chapter. Online courses, podcasts, workshops, and even good old-fashioned books are all available to keep your curiosity piqued and your skills sharp. So, why not treat yourself to a little learning spree?

As you foster your curiosity and commit to lifelong learning, don't forget to share your discoveries with your team. Think of it as a game of knowledge tag; when one person learns something new, they pass it on, and before you know it, everyone is running around with fresh ideas. Encourage your colleagues to embrace their inner detectives too. Host brainstorming sessions where no idea is too wild, and let curiosity lead the charge. You might even create a culture where everyone feels comfortable asking the dumb questions, because let's face it, sometimes the "dumb" questions are the ones that spark the best conversations.

In the end, staying curious is not just a nifty trick for personal growth; it's a fundamental strategy for long-term success. With Customer Experience, where change is the only constant, curiosity is your best ally. Wear your curiosity like a badge of honor. Ask questions, seek answers, and learn continuously. You might just find the secret to not only delighting your customers but also enjoying the ride. In the grand adventure of business, staying curious ensures that the journey is as fun as the destination.

Chapter 10 | Reinforcing Some Ideas: Prioritize CX Leadership

Do It Right or Don't Bother

It's 2011. The final *Harry Potter* movie is tearing up the box office. Adele's *Rolling in the Deep* and LMFAO's *Party Rock Anthem* are dominating the charts. Apple has just released the iPhone 4S, a bittersweet moment less than ten days after the passing of Steve Jobs. Richard Branson opened the first commercial spaceport, bringing space tourism one step closer to reality. And then there was Netflix… making a bit of a blunder.

What happened? Netflix, in all its glory and innovation, made a critical mistake that year. They started using customer survey results as a leading indicator of customer churn. Now, if you're a CX professional, that statement alone probably made you cringe a little. Because here's the thing: customer surveys are great, but they're not leading indicators, they're *lagging* ones. They measure how customers feel *after the fact*. It's like looking at your rearview mirror to figure out where to go. Netflix missed that memo, and it cost them, big time.

They lost 800,000 subscribers that year. Their stock price tanked, plummeting by a brutal 77%. The public relations fallout was severe, with the media and customers alike questioning the management's decision-making. It was a wake-up call. Had they empowered the right CX leaders – leaders with the authority to make strategic decisions based on customer behavior, they might have avoided that epic fallout.

Why CX Should Be a Priority

If there's one thing you should take away from this book, it's this: *Customer Experience is not a department; it's a business-wide responsibility.* And yet, so many companies make the mistake of burying CX management under layers of other functions or departments. They delegate it to people who are miles away from the CEO's Office, leaving the people who understand the customer most with very little influence over the company's overall direction.

That's not just a mistake, it's a missed opportunity.
Think about it. *Who are the people most essential to the survival of your business?* Spoiler alert: it's your customers. Without them, you wouldn't have a business. So why, then, do companies fail to prioritize the leadership role responsible for understanding and delivering value to those customers?

What you need is a *Chief Customer Officer (CCO) or Chief Experience Officer (CXO)* reporting directly to the CEO. There needs to be a short, clear line of communication between your top CX leader and the captain of the ship. Why? Because customers are your business. And without someone advocating for them in the highest levels of decision-making, you're leaving money, loyalty, and growth on the table.

The Netflix Lesson: Lagging Indicators Are Just That – Lagging

Back to Netflix in 2011. Their mistake wasn't just a PR nightmare, it was an operational one. They relied on customer survey results to predict churn. But here's the thing: by the time a customer fills out a survey, it's already too late. They've already experienced your service or product, formed their opinions, and in many cases, made their decision to leave or stay.

Customer survey results are a lagging indicator – they only tell you how customers feel after the fact. By the time you collect that data, analyze it, and make strategic changes, you're already reacting, rather than being proactive.

This is why CX leadership is so critical. A CCO or CXO wouldn't just rely on surveys. They'd be equipped to gather and interpret real-time data from various touchpoints – website interactions, customer support feedback, buying patterns, and more – to make decisions that prevent churn *before* it happens. They wouldn't just tell the CEO, "Hey, we lost a bunch of customers." They'd be able to say, "Here's what our customers are struggling with right now, and here's how we can fix it before we lose them."

CX Leadership Needs to Be at the Table

So, why do we need CX leadership front and center in the boardroom? The answer is simple: *Customer Experience drives business outcomes.* CX leaders don't just help make customers happy; they drive customer retention, loyalty, and revenue growth. The data backs this up. Companies with a strong CX leader are significantly more likely to record higher customer satisfaction, greater loyalty, and yes, a bigger bottom line.

Here's what a strong CX leader does:
1. **Defines the company's customer-centric vision**: They help shape the company's strategy around customer needs. This includes identifying who the target customers are, understanding their challenges, and ensuring that every department, from marketing to product development, is working toward delivering solutions that those customers value.
2. **Acts as the customer's advocate**: The CX leader brings the voice of the customer (VoC) to every executive meeting, sharing key insights and making sure that customer needs are not just heard but prioritized. This is particularly critical when you're making big business decisions like launching a new product, expanding into new markets, or changing pricing structures.
3. **Drives innovation**: A great CX leader doesn't just fix problems, they innovate. They identify new opportunities to improve the customer experience,

whether that's through developing new products, adding services, or leveraging technology to streamline the customer journey.

Why CX Leaders Need Authority and Influence

If you want real results from your CX efforts, if you want to see tangible ROI, your CX leader needs to have the resources and influence necessary to drive change. They need access to data, tools, technology, and most importantly, a direct line to the CEO. Without this, your CX efforts will be underfunded, undermined, and ultimately ineffective.

The CX leader's role is not just to make customers happy in the short term; it's to ensure long-term success by shaping the company's overall strategy around customer needs. If you bury this role under a mountain of bureaucracy, you might as well not even bother.

The Stakes Are Higher Than Ever

In today's marketplace, customers have more choices than ever. They can switch to a competitor with the swipe of a finger, and they will if they're not happy with their experience. The stakes have never been higher. That's why companies that prioritize CX, and more importantly, empower CX leaders, are the ones that come out on top.

You can't treat Customer Experience as a one-time project or something that runs in the background while you focus on other "more important" business objectives. The truth is, *no matter the business, CX is the business objective.* Everything flows from it. Companies that focus on CX management, CX improvement, and CX innovation are the ones that survive and thrive in this competitive landscape.

Don't Cook CX on the Back Burner

The bottom line is this: CX leadership isn't something you can afford to bury under other functions. It's not an afterthought. It needs to be prioritized, empowered, and woven into the fabric of your organization.

If you're serious about customer retention, growth, and loyalty, then it's time to put CX leadership where it belongs: at the top of your organization, right next to the CEO. Only then will you be able to truly transform your business and ensure lasting success in an increasingly competitive world.

So, what are you waiting for? It's time to give Customer Experience the leadership seat it deserves.

Chapter 11 | A Closer Look at NPS (And What You Should Really Know)

Think Fast! What's NPS?

So, you've done it. Like me, you've finally explained Customer Experience to your dad. He's now proudly telling everyone who'll listen that you're some kind of business wunderkind, all-knowing in the ways of customer satisfaction. Life is good, right?

Well, that's all great until you're cornered by Uncle George (who, by the way, isn't even your real uncle, but let's not go there). He pounces with the kind of enthusiasm that makes you rethink ever attending family events: *"What's your take on NPS?"* He blurts it out, oblivious to the fact that you're currently mid-cupcake at your child's birthday party.

You freeze. Part of you considers saying, "George, it's my kid's party. Let's talk about this next weekend." But the other part, the CX professional part, knows you're not going to back down from a challenge like this. So, you decide to be a good sport and jump in. Welcome to this section's topic: the ins and outs of *Net Promoter Score,* or NPS.

NPS: The Basics

It was 2013, and a well-known auto oil change company, to be kind, let's call it *Spiffy Lube,* was in serious trouble. For a decade, they had been making headlines for all the wrong reasons: shoddy service, angry customers, you name it. Desperate to turn things around, they decided to go all-in on the Net Promoter Score method.

Now, whether you've heard the term *NPS* or not, chances are you've encountered it in action. If you've ever bought something, especially online, you've probably been hit with a question like this: *"How likely are you to recommend our company to a friend or colleague?"*

That's NPS in a nutshell.

First proposed by Fred Reichheld in a 2003 article for the Harvard Business Review, NPS has since become a staple metric in the world of customer loyalty. The concept is simple: customers rate their likelihood of recommending a company on a scale from 0 to 10, where 0 is "extremely unlikely" and 10 is "extremely likely."

And if you're like most of us, you've seen this question more times than you care to admit. Sometimes, you even respond. Look at you being an engaged customer! But here's where it gets interesting: NPS scores don't just tell companies how likely you are to recommend them; they group you into one of three categories based on your response:

- **Promoters (9-10)**: You're loyal, satisfied, and ready to sing the company's praises. You're essentially DJ Khaled, but instead of shouting "Another one!" every time you see a good deal, you're likely to repurchase and recommend the company to friends and family.
- **Passives (7-8)**: You're satisfied, but let's not get too excited. You'll use the product, but you're not rushing to tell anyone about it. And if something better comes along, you're not emotionally invested enough to stick around.
- **Detractors (0-6)**: Uh-oh. You're not just dissatisfied, you're angry. And not only are you never coming back, but you're probably going to warn anyone who will listen to stay away. You're telling everyone that the company is a hot mess.

NPS is calculated by subtracting the percentage of **Detractors** from the percentage of **Promoters**. So, for example, if 30% of customers are Promoters and 30% are Detractors, you've got yourself an NPS of 0. Not exactly a number you'd want to brag about.

But even if your NPS is positive, here's the million-dollar question: How reliable is it?

When NPS Goes Wrong: The Spiffy Lube Disaster

Back to Spiffy Lube. In the wake of their bad press, the company became obsessed with improving their NPS. They started offering customers discounts and freebies in exchange for higher survey scores. And guess what? It worked! Their NPS started creeping up. High fives all around, right?

Not so fast.

You see, Spiffy Lube's focus on the *score* distracted them from the actual problems driving their bad reputation. Sure, they got better survey results, but the underlying issues causing customer dissatisfaction were still very much alive and kicking. The quick wins that temporarily boosted their NPS didn't translate into real improvements in service quality. Before long, the cracks began to show – *again*. Sales stagnated, customer churn continued, and they found themselves right back where they started. Turns out, boosting your NPS by bribing customers or manipulating the data doesn't fix the core problems in your business. Who would've thought?

The Dangers of Misusing NPS

Now, let's dig into some common pitfalls when it comes to NPS:
1. **Manipulating the Score**: Like Spiffy Lube, some companies will go to great lengths to push their NPS higher, even if it means offering incentives or only seeking feedback from customers who are likely to

give glowing reviews. But this leads to skewed data and gives leadership a false sense of security. Your score might look good, but the customer experience could still be in shambles.
2. **Ignoring Context**: An NPS score tells you *what* customers think, but it doesn't always tell you *why*. For example, if your Detractors are complaining about price, you might feel compelled to lower prices to appease them. But what if the real issue isn't price, but the perceived value of your product? Simply slashing prices could do more harm than good if it doesn't address the deeper problems.
3. **Oversimplification**: You can't reduce customer loyalty to a single number. NPS doesn't capture the nuances behind customer sentiment, and that's a problem. For instance, a customer might give you a 7 out of 10 because they're generally happy, but that number doesn't reveal the specific areas where your business could improve. You need to dig deeper than the score.

The Complexities of Customer Feedback

Let's talk about a few factors that could impact NPS responses:
- **Customers with Extreme Emotions**: Customers who respond to NPS surveys tend to be either really happy or really upset. Those who are neutral might not bother to respond at all. This means your data could be skewed by the most extreme opinions,

rather than reflecting the full range of customer experiences.
- **Transient Factors**: A customer's score can be affected by transient factors. If they're having a bad day, they just might give you a lower score than you deserve. On the flip side, if they're lounging on a yacht with a cold drink in hand, they might be feeling extra generous. The score you receive may not always reflect their overall sentiment toward your brand.
- **Cultural Differences**: A 7 or 8 out of 10 might be considered a great score in some cultures, but according to NPS, that's still classified as Passive. Most of us have had at least one teacher who said they would never give a perfect score as a matter of principle. Different regions and cultures might interpret the scale differently, which can impact your overall NPS and how you should interpret it.

What Spiffy Lube Learned (The Hard Way)

The story of Spiffy Lube doesn't end with a crashed NPS and lost customers. In 2017, after several years of trying to play the NPS game, the company finally realized that they were focusing on the wrong thing. Instead of obsessing over their score, they shifted their focus back to improving the actual quality of their service.

They invested in training their employees and building a more customer-centric culture. Instead of bribing customers for better survey results, they concentrated on fixing the root problems causing dissatisfaction. The result? Slowly but surely, they turned things around. Customers started coming back, and the company's reputation improved.

The Moral of the Story: Use NPS, But Don't Let It Use You

So, what's the takeaway here? NPS is an incredibly useful tool, but it's not a silver bullet. You need to use it in conjunction with other methods to truly understand your customers. Dig deeper into the data. Look beyond the numbers to find out what your customers are really saying. And most importantly, don't let a high NPS score lull you into a false sense of security. Even Reichheld, the creator of NPS, has acknowledged that companies are often guilty of misusing the score. He's even said that we need to evolve beyond NPS to find better ways of measuring customer loyalty and experience. And if the guy who invented NPS is saying that, you'd be wise to listen.

Oh, and by the time you've finished explaining all of this to Uncle George, he'll either be thoroughly impressed or, more likely, already backed off into the hedges Homer Simpson style and can now be found leading the electric slide in the center of the lawn. Either way, you've done your job. Congratulations.

Chapter 12 | Securing Stakeholder Allyship, Because Even Superman Is Part of a League

Don't Get Stuck Going Nowhere Fast

Well done! You've just started as the new Customer Experience Leader for a company that, until now, has been comfortably ignoring CX. They're proud of themselves for hiring you, and you're excited to hit the ground running. But as the honeymoon phase fades, you start to get that sinking feeling that you've been hired just to add "We're All About CX!" to the company's branding without anyone actually caring about it.

As you navigate through your first few weeks, it becomes clear: the other leaders don't see CX as a priority. They're focused on their own silos, and improving the customer journey isn't even on their radar. If you want to succeed in this role, and actually make a difference, you'll need to start with them. But how do you get a room full of executives to care about CX when it's never been part of their agenda?

When CX Is Not a Priority (Yet)

Remember back in 2014 when Satya Nadella became the CEO of Microsoft? One of the first things he did was drive a vision of *customer obsession*. According to Brad Anderson, a former VP at Microsoft, whenever you went in to talk with Nadella, you had to start with a very simple but powerful question: "What's the customer problem? What are they trying to solve?"

For Nadella, CX wasn't a side project, it was at the very core of Microsoft's business strategy. And it paid off. Microsoft's market cap soared, and the company became more customer-centric across every department.

Now, it's great if your CEO is already aboard with CX train, as Nadella was. But let's be real, most of us don't have the luxury of starting with such significant top-down support. In most cases, you're more than a few rungs below the captain. So how do you, as the CX leader, ensure that Customer Experience becomes a top priority across the entire organization, starting with your executive team?

WIIFM: What's In It For Me?

Here's the first rule of securing stakeholder buy-in: *Nobody cares what you know*. I know, that sounds harsh, but stick with me. It's not that your colleagues don't respect you or your expertise, it's that they care about their own goals first. They're already juggling a thousand priorities. The last thing they want is for someone to come in and tell them to add CX to their ever-growing to-do list. So, you need to flip the conversation.

Every stakeholder, whether it's your CFO, COO, or Head of Sales, is subconsciously asking one thing: *What's In It For Me? (WIIFM)*. Your job is to answer that question in a way that resonates with them.

- **For the CFO**, talk dollars and cents. Show them exactly how much the company is losing due to poor customer retention and churn. Use data to highlight the untapped revenue from increased customer loyalty, upsell potential, and longer Customer Lifetime Value (CLV). Explain how improving CX can reduce customer acquisition costs, drive down churn, and boost profitability.
- **For the Head of Sales**, show them how improving the customer journey can lead to stronger referrals and repeat business. Make it clear that happier customers = easier sales. And for those in sales, anything that makes hitting targets easier is worth investing in.
- **For the COO**, focus on operational efficiencies. Explain how a better Customer Experience reduces customer support tickets, increases process efficiency, and ultimately creates a smoother, more scalable business model.

Tailor your approach to each stakeholder's WIIFM, and you'll start to see their ears perk up.

Back It Up with Data (Leave the Inspirational Speeches at Home)

Now, I know it's tempting to walk into the boardroom armed with nothing but passion, determination, and maybe a motivational quote about how customer obsession is the future. But here's the thing: nobody's buying it. At least, not until you back it up with facts.

Data speaks. To get your stakeholders on board, you need to show them the hard numbers. To name just a few, you can lead with
- **Customer Churn**: What is your company's current churn rate, and what's driving it? If you can calculate how much each lost customer is costing the company, you've suddenly got their attention. If the company loses 10% of its customers annually, calculate the revenue being left on the table.
- **Customer Lifetime Value (CLV)**: Show the projected growth that comes from increasing customer retention. For example, a 5% increase in retention could lead to a 25-95% increase in profits (depending on the industry). Numbers like that make people sit up and listen.
- **Voice of the Customer (VoC)**: Use feedback from customers to highlight pain points. Don't just say, "Customers are frustrated with our product delivery." Show the data. Use customer satisfaction scores, survey results, or social media feedback. Let your customers make the case for you.

Identify Your Champions

In every organization, there are people who just *get it*. They're the ones who understand why CX matters without needing a 20-minute PowerPoint presentation. These are your champions. Find them.
Whether it's a department head, an executive, or even a manager, identify the people who already buy into the idea of CX and leverage their influence to help you spread the message. If the CEO isn't the one driving customer obsession (yet), your champions can act as ambassadors, helping you get more stakeholders on board.

But here's the catch: you can't do it alone. Even the most passionate CX leader will hit roadblocks if they don't have the right allies. In any successful change-management strategy, the key is not just identifying stakeholders but empowering them to help lead the charge.

Make Them Part of the Solution

Now that you've got their attention, the last thing you want to do is present them with a fully-baked CX strategy and ask them to sign off on it. Why? Because when people feel like they didn't have a hand in creating something, they're less invested in making sure it succeeds.

Instead of just presenting your CX strategy, *involve your stakeholders* in the process. Ask for their input. Make them feel like co-creators. After all, they're the ones who will be overseeing the execution of these initiatives in their respective departments. The more ownership they feel, the more likely they are to support and champion CX initiatives long after the meetings end.

Here are some ways to involve them:

- **Workshops**: Host cross-functional workshops where different teams collaborate on CX initiatives. Give each department a voice in the strategy.
- **Pilot Programs**: Instead of rolling out CX changes company-wide, start with pilot programs. Get buy-in from one or two departments to test new initiatives, then use the success of those programs to build momentum.
- **Regular Check-ins**: Don't let CX be a one-and-done conversation. Schedule regular check-ins with stakeholders to review progress, discuss challenges, and celebrate wins. Keep the dialogue open, and make sure they're engaged throughout the process.

The Bottom Line: CX Requires Collective Ownership

Here's the truth: no matter how passionate you are about CX, *you can't do it alone.* You're one person. One leader. And no matter how great your strategy is, if the rest of your organization doesn't care about it, nothing will change.

To succeed, you need everyone, from the executive team to the front-line employees, thinking and acting in customer-centric ways. And that starts with securing buy-in from your key stakeholders. If they're not invested, your CX strategy is dead in the water before it even begins.

So, remember: when it comes to CX leadership, *the power isn't in knowing more than everyone else, it's in getting everyone else to care as much as you do.* Find your champions. Speak their language. Back it up with data. And get them involved in co-creating a strategy that they feel ownership over.

Because if you're the only one who cares about Customer Experience, nothing's going to happen. And that, my friend, would be a damn shame.

Chapter 13 | EX & CX From 30,000ft, Without the Vertigo

Are Employees Really a Big Deal?

Let's start with a name that commands attention: Sir Richard Branson. You know the guy – founder of the Virgin Group, serial entrepreneur, and all-around business legend. Branson has dropped some pretty iconic lines over the years, but there's one in particular that resonates deeply in the world of Customer Experience:

"Clients do not come first. Employees come first. If you take care of your employees, they will take care of the clients."

Now, if you're scratching your head at first, don't worry, you're not alone. It's one of those statements that seems counterintuitive at first blush. *Isn't the customer always supposed to come first? Isn't that Business 101? Also, didn't you literally say that earlier in this book? Make up your mind, man!* I hear you.

But let's unpack what Branson's really getting at. Because here's the thing: taking care of your employees is the foundation for taking care of your customers. And once you understand this concept, you'll see why Employee Experience (EX) and Customer Experience (CX) are two sides of the same coin.

The Employee-Customer Connection: What Branson Knows That Many Don't

Branson isn't just saying this because it sounds good. It's not a fluff statement for motivational posters. He's learned, from years of running a global empire, that *happy employees make for happy customers.*

Here's another Branson gem:

"By putting the employee first, the customer effectively comes first by default, and in the end, the shareholder comes first by default as well."

That too might sound a little convoluted at first, but once you get the logic, it's crystal clear. If your employees are empowered, engaged, and treated well, they'll naturally extend that positivity to the customers they interact with or impact. This, in turn, drives customer loyalty, retention, and ultimately profits, which is exactly what your shareholders want.

So, when you take care of your employees, you're indirectly taking care of both your customers and your shareholders. Pretty efficient, right?

Why Employee Experience (EX) Matters to CX

Let's rewind for a second and look at this through a broader lens. In a previous chapter, I mentioned that in today's increasingly competitive business landscape, you need to be the best at delivering value to your customers if you want to survive. That's why you care about CX. Because better experiences lead to customer retention, renewals, and growth.

But here's the secret: *you can't deliver a top-notch Customer Experience without first mastering the Employee Experience.* EX is the sum of all interactions an employee has with your organization, from recruitment to exit. It covers everything from onboarding to development, and how well you retain them.

Why does this matter to CX? Because unless you're running a one-person operation (and even then), you're relying on people across your company to deliver your products or services to customers. Those people, the ones in Marketing, Customer Service, IT, and all the other departments, are the ones responsible for your customers' *Jobs-To-Be-Done (JTBD)*. You're trusting each and every one of them to do their part in making sure your customers' needs are met.

And let's be real: they're not going to be at their best if they feel undervalued, uninspired, or stuck using outdated tools.

So if you want your customers to be happy, you first need to make sure your employees are happy.

Maslow's Hierarchy, But for Employees

We all know Maslow's Hierarchy of Needs – the psychological theory that humans need to meet their basic survival needs before they can focus on self-actualization. Well, a similar idea applies to your employees. If their basic needs, like fair pay, decent working conditions, and proper tools, aren't being met, how can you expect them to deliver at their highest level? You can't expect your employees to be inspired, creative problem-solvers for your customers if their own needs aren't being met. If they're frustrated by poor management, hampered by antiquated technology, or disillusioned with company culture, those frustrations are going to spill over into their interactions with customers.

And here's the truth: *happy employees lead to happy customers.* According to a study by Gallup, companies with engaged employees outperform their competition by a whopping **147%**. Yes, you read that right. Nearly **150% better** performance. Engaged employees are more productive, more innovative, and more committed to delivering great results for your customers. That, in turn, leads to better customer satisfaction, loyalty, and ultimately higher revenue.

But employee engagement and satisfaction don't happen by magic. You need an *intentional EX strategy* to create the right environment for your team to thrive.

The Three Environments That Impact EX

Let's turn to Jacob Morgan, the author of *The Employee Experience Advantage*. According to Morgan, there are three environments that impact Employee Experience:

1. Company Culture
2. Technology Environment
3. Workplace Environment

These three pillars shape how employees experience your organization. Let's break them down.

- **Company Culture**: This is the emotional and social fabric of your organization. Does your culture foster collaboration, respect, and innovation? Or is it a toxic, high-pressure environment where employees feel expendable? Culture shapes how employees feel about their work, their colleagues, and their ability to contribute meaningfully to the company's success.
- **Technology Environment**: The tools your employees use every day are critical. Antiquated or ill-suited tools create inefficiencies, frustration, and ultimately, burnout. If your employees are stuck using outdated software or clunky systems, it's only

a matter of time before that frustration seeps into their interactions with customers. Invest in modern, efficient tools, and you'll see the difference it makes in both EX and CX.
- **Workplace Environment**: This includes the physical space where your employees work. Is it a space that encourages collaboration and focus? Is it conducive to creativity and problem-solving? In today's world, workplace environment also includes flexible working arrangements like remote work. Providing the right physical (or virtual) space for your employees to thrive is crucial for their overall experience.

The Cost of Ignoring EX

Ignoring EX is like trying to fill a leaking bucket. You can keep pouring in new employees, but if the Employee Experience is poor, they'll leave just as fast as they arrive. And every time an employee leaves, they take with them valuable company-specific knowledge, relationships, and skills. This constant churn stunts your company's growth because you're always stuck at the starting line, never able to build on the institutional knowledge of a stable, experienced workforce.

The cost of employee turnover is astronomical, not just in recruitment and onboarding expenses but in lost productivity and morale. If your company becomes a revolving door, your customers will notice, and they won't stick around, either.

You Can't Give What You Don't Have

That's right, you can't give what you don't have. If your employees don't feel inspired, empowered, or engaged, how can you expect them to inspire, empower, and engage your customers? Your customer-facing employees aren't the only ones involved in Customer Experience. *Everyone in your company is a part of the CX ecosystem,* whether they interact with customers directly or not.

And that brings us back to Branson's wisdom: Take care of your employees, and they'll take care of your customers. It's that straightforward.

The Bottom Line: EX Drives CX

If you want to deliver a standout Customer Experience, you need to start by investing in your Employee Experience. It's not just a feel-good strategy, it's a competitive advantage. When you create an environment where employees are happy, engaged, and equipped to do their best work, you create a natural ripple effect that extends to your customers.

Richard Branson said it best: *"An exceptional company is the one that gets all the little details right. And the people out on the front line, they know when things are not going right, and they know when things need to be improved. And if you listen to them, you can soon improve all those niggly things which turn an average company into an exceptional company."*

Understand that every employee is on the front line of CX, even those who never interact directly with customers. Empower them, listen to them, and give them the tools and environment they need to thrive. Do this, and your employees will go the extra mile to make sure your customers are happy.

Because at the end of the day, if you're not taking care of the people who take care of your customers, how can you expect to grow, retain, and delight those customers? It's clear: Take care of your employees, and they will take care of your customers.

Chapter 14 | CX Operations & CX Engagement: The Property Brothers or Jekyll & Hyde?

A Package Deal for Success

During a casual conversation, a friend asked me about a certain industry leader who seemed to have an intense focus on *CX Operations,* but barely gave a second thought to *CX Engagement.* Their question: "Is this approach sustainable?" My answer: Nope.

It's 1971. A college student named Steve Wozniak meets a high-schooler named Steve Jobs. They instantly click, bonding over their mutual love of electronics and a shared enthusiasm for pranks. This quirky friendship eventually blossoms into one of the most iconic partnerships in business history, giving birth to Apple, one of the world's most valuable companies.

Now, let's imagine a world where only one of the Steves existed. Would Apple have still been as successful without both of them? Maybe, but I wouldn't bet on it. They were a dynamic duo, each bringing different strengths to the table. Jobs, with his vision for design and marketing, brought customer engagement to life, while Wozniak's engineering genius built the operational backbone. Without the two working in tandem, there would be no Apple as we know it.

And in the same way, there can be no CX excellence without a balance between CX Operations and CX Engagement.

CX Engagement: The Emotional Connection

First, let's break down CX Engagement. This refers to the touchpoints and strategies that create meaningful, memorable interactions with customers. It's the face of your company, the part that customers interact with, and the emotional connection they build with your brand.

Think about it: Every time a customer places an order, contacts customer service, visits your website, or interacts with your social media, they are experiencing CX Engagement. It's not just about solving problems; it's about *creating moments of delight* that make customers feel valued. These interactions foster loyalty and build the emotional connection that keeps customers coming back.

Good CX Engagement makes the customer feel like they're in good hands. It's why you keep going back to your favorite coffee shop or why you'd rather wait a few extra days for delivery from your go-to retailer. You're emotionally invested in the brand because they've created a *relationship*, not just a transaction.

CX Operations: The Engine That Powers Engagement

None of that delightful engagement is possible without CX Operations. Behind every seamless customer experience is a well-oiled machine of backend systems, processes, and infrastructure. CX Operations are the foundation that supports everything customers see on the front end.

Imagine ordering a product from a company with fantastic customer service and engaging social media, only to find that your delivery arrives late, or worse, never shows up at all. Suddenly, that glowing engagement falls flat because the operations behind it failed to deliver. It's like having the flashiest, most polished website but no product behind it to sell.

CX Operations is the part of your company that ensures that the promises made during CX Engagement are actually delivered. It's everything from inventory management, order fulfillment, and ticketing systems to process standardization and quality control. Without solid operations in place, even the most well-intentioned engagement strategy will collapse under the weight of unmet customer expectations.

The Symbiotic Relationship: Engagement Informs Operations

The relationship between CX Operations and CX Engagement is symbiotic; one doesn't work without the other. Take Amazon, for example. Their CX Engagement is world-class. When you visit their site, you're hit with personalized recommendations that feel like the platform knows you better than you know yourself. But behind those engaging moments is a robust backend of CX Operations: cutting-edge inventory management, predictive analytics, and a logistics system that ensures your order arrives when you expect it to. What makes Amazon stand out isn't just its flashy engagement strategies, but the fact that its operations enable and support those engagements. The magic is in the way Amazon marries both sides of CX, engagement and operations, to create an experience that feels almost effortless for the customer.

But it's not just tech giants like Amazon that benefit from this balance. Even smaller companies can use insights gathered from CX Engagement to inform and refine their operations. For example, a software company receiving regular feedback from customers about frequent download interruptions can decide to invest more resources in their backend infrastructure. Fixing this operational issue will then elevate the overall customer experience.

Consistency Is King

In CX, *consistency is key*. Consistent CX Operations ensure that the quality of CX Engagement remains high across all customer touchpoints, all the time. Let me give you an example you've probably experienced:

Think about Starbucks. You walk in, order your usual vanilla latte, and expect it to taste the same whether you're in Los Angeles, Toronto, or a tiny town in the middle of nowhere. The magic behind that consistency? CX Operations. Starbucks has perfected its backend processes, from bean roasting to barista training, to ensure that every cup is the same high quality no matter where you are.

If Starbucks didn't have rock-solid CX Operations, customers would be playing a game of roulette every time they ordered. And if that happened, they'd lose trust in the brand, no matter how friendly the baristas are or how great the playlist is. That's CX Engagement failing because CX Operations couldn't support it.

The Property Brothers of CX: Engagement & Operations Working Together

Here's how I like to think of it: CX Operations and CX Engagement are like the Property Brothers. It's not the Property Brothers without both brothers. It's not CX

Excellence without both CX Operations and CX Engagement. One is great at envisioning the finished product and making it beautiful (that's Engagement), while the other gets into the nitty-gritty of the structure, making sure it doesn't collapse (that's Operations).

A business that only focuses on CX Engagement without proper CX Operations is like designing a beautiful house with no foundation. Sure, it looks great, until it crumbles. On the flip side, focusing only on CX Operations without engaging the customer will leave your business feeling like an efficient machine with no soul. No one wants to live in a house that's functional but sterile.

Just like Jobs and Wozniak, CX Engagement and CX Operations need to work together. Operations support the engagement efforts, making sure every interaction is smooth and reliable. In return, Engagement provides insights that can help Operations improve and innovate.

So, as you think about your own business, ask yourself: Are you balancing both sides of the equation?

Chapter 15 | Change Management for Adopting Customer-Centricity (Part 1)

The Struggle of Change – Even When It's Good

We've all been there. We know someone, heck, maybe we *are* someone, who finds change difficult. Even when the change is positive, even when it's something they've been working toward, the mere process of shifting from one state to another can bring out all kinds of resistance.

And if you think it's hard for one person to manage change, imagine how complex it gets when you scale that up to an entire organization. People, processes, tools – all pieces of the puzzle, each with their own reactions to change. Now, throw in a fundamental shift like adopting customer-centricity, and you've got yourself one heck of a transition.

There's no shortage of stories in pop culture and history about people who seemed to self-sabotage after achieving success. We've all seen it: wildly talented individuals who, after pulling themselves up to great heights, somehow manage to derail their own progress just when things are going well.

Why does this happen? What is it about change, even positive change, that makes us so uncomfortable? Some people just have a hard time adapting, even to the things they've worked so hard for. And let's be honest, it's easy to judge from the outside looking in. We say, "How could they mess up after getting this far?" But the truth is, change, no matter how beneficial, brings with it a host of uncertainties, and uncertainty can feel like a threat.

This phenomenon isn't unique to individuals. Companies can be just as guilty of self-sabotage when it comes to making critical changes. The idea of switching to a customer-centric model might sound fantastic on paper, but in practice, it requires a radical shift in mindset, behavior, and infrastructure. It's no wonder so many companies stumble when they try to implement it.

But here's the thing: *customer-centricity is not optional.* In today's market, customers are in the driver's seat. They have endless options, and their expectations have never been higher. That's why change management is so crucial when transitioning to a customer-centric model. Without it, your business risks faltering at the very moment it should be thriving.

So, What Is Customer-Centricity, Really?

Before we dive into change management, let's get clear on what we mean by customer-centricity. One of my favorite definitions is that it's the strategy of putting the customer at the center of everything your organization does. It's not a slogan you slap onto your next marketing campaign or a box you check in your annual report. It's about understanding your customers' needs and expectations and then aligning every part of your organization – people, processes, tools, products, services – around meeting those needs.

Customer-centric businesses are constantly looking for ways to improve the customer experience. They listen to feedback. They evolve. They're never satisfied with just "good enough," because they know that satisfied customers = long-term success.

And that's why you, old friend, care about customer-centricity. You care because it leads to greater customer satisfaction, loyalty, and referrals. It attracts new customers, helps you retain the ones you've already got, and provides a serious competitive advantage. In short, it's a sure-fire way to boost sales and profits.

But becoming customer-centric isn't about tossing out some feel-good messages about how you love your customers. It's about getting serious. It requires real, intentional effort that seeps into every aspect of your business. It's about reshaping your company's DNA so that customer satisfaction becomes not just a goal but *the goal*. And trust me, that kind of shift is no small feat.

The Pain of Changing Mindsets

Here's the kicker: For many employees, this means changing how they think about their jobs. In a customer-centric organization, every single role is tied to the customer in some way. Whether you're in Product Development, Marketing, IT, or Finance, you need to be thinking about *how your work impacts the customer.*

For some, this will be a massive shift. They'll have to learn new skills, like customer listening, problem-solving, and maybe even empathy. They'll need to start seeing the customer not as a vague, abstract concept but as the very reason their role exists. And, if they've never been asked to think this way before, there's a good chance they'll push back.

Tools and Processes: Fit for Purpose or Cramping Style?

And it's not just about changing minds. Tools and processes are going to need an overhaul, too. Every system in your company needs to be run through a gauntlet of radical evaluation to see if it's still fit for purpose. And what's that purpose? *Customer focus.* If your tools and processes don't align with your customer-centric mission, it's time to upgrade. That might mean implementing new CRM systems, rethinking your supply chain, or adopting more customer-friendly technologies.

Here's the rub: *If not properly managed, these changes can break your company.* That's right. Go too fast, and you risk overwhelming your people and crashing your operations. Go too slow, and you'll lag behind the competition and frustrate your customers. Upset the wrong stakeholders, and the entire initiative could be dead in the water before it even gets started.

The Game-Changer: Change Management

This is where Change management comes in. Change Management is the structured process of transitioning individuals, teams, and organizations from their current state to a desired future state. It's a methodical approach to getting from "here" to "there" without losing everything along the way.

Change Management covers everything from preparation and planning to execution and, most importantly, resolution. You don't just dive into a customer-centric model and hope for the best. You lay the groundwork, address the resistance, and guide your team through every step of the process.

The Perils of Not Having a Plan

Without Change Management, adopting customer-centricity is like diving into the deep end of the pool without knowing how to swim. Maybe you'll figure it out before you drown. Or maybe not.

The key is balance. You can't rush this transformation, but you also can't drag your feet. Upsetting the wrong people, failing to communicate effectively, or not adequately training your team could spell disaster. Imagine how quickly a poorly-executed transformation could go sideways – customer dissatisfaction, operational chaos, and employee burnout.

Real talk: Change is hard, even when it's positive. So, how do you manage this transformation smoothly?

The Road Ahead

Next, we'll dive deeper into the *how* of Change Management. We'll talk about the strategies and tools that will guide your organization through this transition and ensure that your journey toward customer-centricity is a success.

Customer-centricity is a powerful goal, but it's also a monumental shift for any organization. To get there, you'll need a thoughtful, structured approach. Change Management isn't just another buzzword, it's your lifeline as you guide your company through this transformation. In the next chapter, we'll look at how to get it right, avoid common pitfalls, and build a strategy that turns customer-centricity from a lofty ideal into a tangible reality.

Chapter 16 | Change Management for Adopting Customer-Centricity (Part 2)

Mapping Out a Plan of Action: From Ideas to Results

In the last chapter, we dug deeper into the concept of customer-centricity – the *why* behind this fundamental change. After receiving zero reports of readers falling asleep halfway through (thanks, guys!), we're ready to take things a step further. Now, we're tackling the *how* – the part where all those great intentions meet the messy reality of organizational change.

If you're reading this, you've probably made the bold decision that customer-centricity is the way forward for your company. Congratulations! Now comes the real challenge: guiding your entire organization through this change without breaking everything. Let's map out a strategy for getting from point A (where you are now) to point B (where customer-centricity is ingrained in your company's DNA).

1. Establish the Need for Change

Your first job is to make the case for why this change is necessary. Your people already have enough on their plates without having to worry about yet another initiative. They need to see that this isn't just a flavor-of-the-month trend but a genuine, strategic shift that will benefit both them and the company.

To do this, show how the company is underperforming by highlighting the costs of missed, misunderstood, and unmet customer needs. Use concrete examples, data, and real-world cases that everyone can understand and relate to. For example, if your company is losing customers faster than it's gaining them, or if customer satisfaction scores are down, quantify that impact in financial terms. When people understand what's at stake, they're more likely to get on board.

2. Articulate the Vision for a Customer-Centric Future

Once people understand the need for change, they need a clear picture of what success looks like. Articulate a compelling vision of your customer-centric future. This is where you inspire your team to aim higher. Help them see how a customer-focused approach will elevate not just the company's success, but their own.

Here's the key: Don't just *tell* them what will be different. *Show* them how this change will lead to *greater customer loyalty, stronger sales,* and *enhanced job satisfaction.* When your team understands that customer-centricity doesn't just help customers but benefits everyone, they'll be more motivated to join you on the journey.

3. Align the Organization Behind the Vision

For customer-centricity to take root, every department and team needs to align with this vision. CX isn't the job of one department; it's the responsibility of the entire organization. Sales, Marketing, Product Development, IT, everyone has a role to play in delivering a great customer experience.

Here's how to make that alignment happen:
- **Communicate the Vision Clearly**: Make sure the organization's CX mission, vision, and goals are communicated and understood at every level. Every employee should know not just the *what* but also the *why* behind customer-centricity.
- **Tie Objectives to Customer Outcomes**: Ensure that every department has goals tied to customer outcomes. Sales, for example, might focus on increasing customer retention, while IT might prioritize uptime and efficiency. When every department is working toward a customer-centric goal, the vision becomes tangible.

4. Identify Stakeholders and Overcome Resistance

In any organization, stakeholders will be at different levels of readiness for change. Some will be excited; others, not so much. Identifying your key stakeholders early on allows you to address resistance proactively. Show each stakeholder group *what's in it for them*. Perhaps adopting a customer-centric approach will make the Sales team's job easier or improve operational efficiency for the Logistics team. Customize your messaging to resonate with each group's unique needs.

Once you've identified the people who "get it," recruit them as allies. *Form a CX Governing Committee* made up of leaders from different departments who are responsible for driving, modeling, and refining the customer-centric culture across the organization. This group becomes the champions of customer focus, responsible for influencing their own teams and helping bring lagging stakeholders up to speed.

5. Develop Skills and Implement New Tools

Transitioning to a customer-centric organization may require new skills and tools. As part of your Change Management strategy, identify any skill gaps and outline a roadmap for upskilling. For instance, if customer-listening and problem-solving aren't strengths across the board, invest in training that strengthens these areas.

Similarly, assess whether the tools you're using are fit for purpose. Do you need a new CRM system? Is your customer feedback loop as efficient as it could be? Map out a plan for onboarding new tools and streamlining old processes. This is an investment in the foundation of customer-centricity, so don't rush it.

6. Maintain Consistency and Measure Progress

Once the wheels are in motion, consistency is your best friend. Organizational change is challenging, and without consistent reinforcement, even the best-intentioned initiatives can fizzle out. Regularly communicate the customer-centric vision and celebrate teams and individuals who embody this mindset.

Implement Key Performance Indicators (KPIs) to measure the progress of each department's efforts in shifting toward customer-centricity. Set clear metrics to track things like customer satisfaction, retention, Net Promoter Score (NPS), and Customer Lifetime Value (CLV). By monitoring progress, you'll be able to pinpoint what's working, adjust what isn't, and ensure that everyone stays on track.

7. Risk Mitigation: Navigating the Hurdles

Change is rarely a smooth process, and any significant transformation carries risks. Maybe there's a risk of overloading your team with too many initiatives at once, or perhaps you're concerned about potential backlash from employees who aren't yet on board.

That's where Risk Mitigation comes in. Keep a close eye on potential pitfalls and have contingency plans in place. For example, if you're rolling out new technology, make sure you've accounted for potential downtime and have a support system ready. If you're concerned about burnout, monitor employee feedback and be prepared to adjust workloads as needed.

Effective risk management doesn't mean you'll avoid every bump in the road, but it does mean you'll be better prepared to handle challenges as they arise.

8. Celebrate Successes Along the Way

Adopting a customer-centric approach is a long journey, and it's crucial to celebrate milestones along the way. People need to see that their efforts are making a difference. Whether it's achieving a new customer satisfaction high, reducing churn, or getting a glowing customer testimonial, take the time to recognize and celebrate these wins.

Publicly acknowledging successes helps keep everyone motivated and reminds your team that even small improvements contribute to the bigger picture. And remember, celebration isn't just about giving kudos, it's about building a culture that values customer focus and shows appreciation for employees who contribute to it.

In Closing: A Launchpad for Transformation

This guide is by no means exhaustive, but it's a solid foundation. Customer-centricity is a long-term commitment, and successful change management is what will get you there. If you're serious about putting customers at the heart of your business, you need to be just as committed to guiding your team through the transformation process.

If you're still with me, it's safe to say you've got the grit and vision to make this change happen. You understand that you can't have a business without customers and that prioritizing their needs isn't just a noble idea, it's essential to success in today's world. Now, with a clear strategy in place, you're ready to lead your organization into a future where customers aren't just a piece of the puzzle, they're the core of everything you do.

So go ahead, take these strategies and build on them. Your customer-centric future is within reach, and change management will be the key to unlocking it.

Chapter 17 | Distinguishing Customer Success from Customer Experience

Similar, But Not the Same

Picture this: you step into a beautifully curated art gallery. The lighting is perfect, the ambiance is just right, and each piece of art is positioned to evoke emotion, contemplation, and perhaps even a bit of wonder. This is *Customer Experience* – the thoughtfully designed, emotionally resonant environment that makes you feel comfortable, intrigued, and engaged. Now, as you wander the gallery, imagine a knowledgeable guide joins you, providing insight, explaining the background and history, and helping you understand each piece on a deeper level. This is *Customer Success* – the support, guidance, and resources that ensure you walk away with more than just a nice visit, but a real understanding and appreciation.

Both Customer Experience and Customer Success play pivotal roles in a well-rounded customer-centric strategy. And while they might seem interchangeable, they each serve unique, complementary functions that ultimately drive a positive and lasting customer relationship. So, what exactly sets them apart? Let's dig into the nuances and see how both together can transform a good experience into an unforgettable one.

Understanding Customer Success

Customer Success is a proactive strategy with one clear focus: *helping customers achieve their goals using your product or service.* It's about deeply understanding the customer's objectives and then aligning your efforts to help them reach those targets, with the long-term aim of building a positive, mutually beneficial relationship.

Customer Success is all about engagement from the start. It's there at onboarding, guiding customers to see the full value of what you offer. Imagine a software company offering robust, complex tools to help businesses manage operations. Without Customer Success, many customers might struggle with onboarding, potentially missing out on key functionalities or abandoning the platform altogether. A strong Customer Success team, on the other hand, would provide training, ongoing support, and resources, helping customers to unlock the software's full potential.

Key elements of Customer Success include:
- **Onboarding and Training**: From the beginning, Customer Success helps customers understand how to use the product to meet their needs.
- **Account Management and Check-ins**: Regular engagement and check-ins allow the company to monitor satisfaction, address any concerns, and ensure that customers continue to derive value.
- **Identifying Value-add Opportunities**: A proactive Customer Success approach might reveal ways to integrate other company products or services that

further enhance the customer's experience, building a relationship based on trust and alignment with customer goals.

Customer Success is especially critical for subscription-based businesses or any service that requires ongoing commitment. Customers are unlikely to renew a service if they don't see clear value, which is why a robust Customer Success strategy is essential for retaining customers and ensuring they reach their desired outcomes.

Defining Customer Experience

Customer Experience encompasses every interaction a customer has with your company, from their first encounter with your website to their most recent interaction with customer support. It includes both qualitative and quantitative aspects: how customers feel about each interaction, and the tangible impacts of those interactions on their perception of your brand.

Consider how you feel when you navigate a website. Is it easy to find what you're looking for? Are the pages responsive? Is it visually engaging, without overwhelming you with pop-ups or intrusive ads? All of these elements contribute to Customer Experience. This holistic view of customer interaction focuses on how customers perceive your brand through each touchpoint, and it's shaped by emotions as much as by function.

Customer Experience aims to create a cohesive and enjoyable journey. Every detail counts, from the language you use in customer communications to the ease of your return policy. When companies focus on Customer Experience, they prioritize consistency, accessibility, and emotional resonance, all in an effort to make customers feel valued and understood.

Where They Intersect: The Synergy of Success and Experience

So, where do Customer Success and Customer Experience overlap? The two are closely intertwined, as each supports and reinforces the other. Let's look at a few ways they interact:

- **Customer Experience Informs Customer Success**: By monitoring Customer Experience at each touchpoint, companies gain valuable insights into pain points and areas where customers may need more support. If customers consistently struggle with a specific feature, for example, Customer Success can step in to provide targeted guidance and resources.
- **Customer Success Enhances Customer Experience**: When Customer Success helps customers reach their goals, it naturally elevates the overall experience. If customers feel they're achieving their desired outcomes and have ongoing support, their perception of the brand improves. This,

in turn, positively impacts Customer Experience across the board.

Imagine using a streaming service that not only offers an extensive library of movies and shows via a stellar app (the experience) but also helps you discover content you love through personalized recommendations (success). This combination of experience and success is what keeps you engaged and coming back for more.

The Functional vs. Emotional Divide

In broad terms, Customer Success focuses on the functional relationship between the customer and the company. It's about providing the right resources, guidance, and tools to ensure the customer derives tangible value from the product or service. Meanwhile, Customer Experience dives into the emotional and perceptual aspects, shaping how customers feel about the brand.

Take, for example, a fitness app. Customer Success involves onboarding users, providing workout plans, and guiding them toward their fitness goals. Customer Experience, on the other hand, includes the app's design, usability, and how it makes the customer feel as they engage with it. Ideally, you want both functional support and an enjoyable, motivating experience.

Building a Customer-Centric Strategy with Both CX and CS

Successful companies recognize that both Customer Success and Customer Experience are essential for a truly customer-centric approach. Here's how to blend them into a cohesive strategy:

1. **Begin with Customer Experience**: Ensure that every touchpoint – your website, app, customer support, and even your email communication – is designed to create a positive, consistent, and intuitive experience.
2. **Layer in Customer Success Early**: Engage customers from the start with a proactive Customer Success model that helps them reach their desired outcomes. By being present from onboarding, you set the tone for a supportive and results-oriented relationship.
3. **Use Customer Experience Insights to Refine Customer Success**: Monitor the customer journey for feedback and adjust your Customer Success strategy based on those insights. If customers report friction points, Customer Success can step in with resources and guidance to smooth things out.
4. **Create a Feedback Loop**: Encourage communication between Customer Experience and Customer Success teams to foster a continuous improvement cycle. The better these teams collaborate, the more effectively they can address customer needs and enhance overall satisfaction.

5. **Invest in Ongoing Development**: Don't treat Customer Success and Customer Experience as one-time initiatives. Continually refine both areas to adapt to evolving customer expectations and new opportunities for growth.

The Value of a Holistic Approach

It's possible to have a Customer Experience strategy without a strong Customer Success focus, but the results won't be nearly as impactful. Customers may have a positive impression of your brand, but without guidance to achieve their goals, they may still churn. Conversely, a great Customer Success strategy without a strong Customer Experience can feel cold and transactional. Customers may achieve their objectives but feel no emotional connection to your brand.

The magic happens when both Customer Success and Customer Experience are woven together, creating a journey that is both functional and enjoyable, both goal-oriented and engaging. This holistic approach not only helps customers achieve their objectives but also fosters a lasting emotional connection, turning satisfied customers into loyal advocates.

So, the next time you think about your customer strategy, ask yourself: Are you curating a beautiful gallery that people love to walk through, while also offering them a rich, guided experience? When you balance the roles of

Customer Success and Customer Experience, you create a customer journey that is immersive, fulfilling, and ultimately unforgettable.

Chapter 18 | Wrapping It Up: What the Fuss *Is* Really All About

You Made It!

Well, here we are! At the end of this book and perhaps just the beginning of a new way of looking at Customer Experience. You've read the stories, dived into the insights, chuckled (hopefully), and maybe even had a few lightbulb moments. But as you close this book, let's recap what the "actual fuss" about CX is, and why it matters so much more than just another corporate buzzword.

CX Is More Than Just a Department, It's a Philosophy

We started with the basics, didn't we? Customer Experience isn't just about customer service or a call center, it's the sum of everything customers feel, see, and touch when they engage with your brand. It's the difference between customers tolerating you and genuinely *loving* you. And let's face it, in a world where there's another option just a click away, you want customers who love you. Anything less? Well, that's a fast track to irrelevance.

Success and Experience Go Hand in Hand

We talked about the dance between Customer Success and Customer Experience, how one supports, uplifts, and complements the other. Sure, you can have a slick, beautiful experience that draws people in, but if they don't find success with your product, they're gone. On the flip side, all the guidance in the world won't keep them if the experience feels like a trip to the dentist who works exclusively with a buzzsaw. Together, these two elements make magic happen. It's like peanut butter and jelly or, for the fancy readers, wine and cheese: individually fine, but together, *chef's kiss*.

Change Management: The Key to Becoming Truly Customer-Centric

Ah, Change Management! Not exactly the most fun part of CX, but it's where the rubber meets the road. We explored why bringing customer-centricity into your organization isn't an overnight flip; it's a shift in culture, processes, and priorities. From establishing a clear vision to involving all departments and handling the inevitable resistance, adopting a CX mindset requires commitment. It's tough work, but the payoff – loyal customers, motivated teams, and a reputation that precedes you – is worth every bit of effort.

Consistency, Feedback, and Continuous Improvement: The Lifeblood of CX

We talked about consistency as the secret ingredient that keeps customers coming back. It's not enough to dazzle them once. Every interaction, from the website to the customer support line, should feel like it's part of one cohesive experience. And let's not forget feedback – the gift that keeps on giving. Listening, improving, and adapting based on what customers tell you creates a cycle of continuous improvement. Staying sharp and responsive is how you keep that competitive edge.

Taking Care of Your Team So They Can Take Care of Your Customers

Last but certainly not least, we looked at Employee Experience (EX) and its impact on CX. Happy employees lead to happy customers. A simple truth, but one that too many businesses overlook. When your team feels valued, supported, and empowered, that positivity spills over to customers in ways you can't fake. Take care of the people who take care of your customers, and you're building a foundation for CX excellence that will weather any storm.

So, Why Does the CX Buzzword Relentlessly Haunt Us?

Here's the big takeaway: Customer Experience isn't going anywhere. It's here to stay, and it's only going to become more central to how businesses operate, differentiate, and grow. The "fuss" isn't just hype; it's the recognition that CX is the frontline in the battle for loyalty, trust, and relevance.

Companies that embrace CX as a core philosophy, not just a department, are the ones who will thrive. They're the ones who will not only attract customers but inspire them, impress them, and keep them coming back. So, the next time you hear someone groaning about "yet another CX initiative," feel free to tell them that the only real "buzzword" is *success*, and CX is the road to get there.

Keep Striving for Customer Excellence

As we come to the final words of this book, I'd like to say thank you for coming on this road trip with me. We've talked about such important things as cavemen and toddlers, cats and fries, and even a little bit of Customer Experience. If you walk away with a deeper appreciation for the power of CX (and maybe a few good laughs), then I've done my job. CX might be complex, but it doesn't have to be dry, and it sure doesn't have to be confusing. It's an ever-evolving adventure, and if you've made it this far, I have a feeling you're ready to tackle it head-on.

My objective has been to inspire you to keep striving to create moments that matter. Keep questioning, keep improving, and most importantly, *keep putting your customers at the heart of everything you do.* And who knows? Maybe we'll run into each other on this road to customer excellence and have a chance to continue this conversation.

Until then, go forth and make some CX magic happen!

Glossary

1. **Amazon**
   A global e-commerce and cloud computing company headquartered in Seattle, Washington. Amazon is known for its customer-centric approach, with innovations like fast delivery, personalized recommendations, and a seamless shopping experience.

2. **Apple**
   An American multinational technology company known for its innovative products, including the iPhone, Mac computers, and software platforms. Apple is recognized for its focus on both Customer Experience and design, creating products that are intuitive and user-friendly.

3. **Brad Anderson**
   A former Vice President at Microsoft who highlighted CEO Satya Nadella's commitment to customer-centricity. Anderson has shared insights on how Nadella emphasizes starting discussions with the customer's perspective.

4. **Change Management**
   A structured approach to transitioning individuals, teams, and organizations to a new state. In CX, change management is essential when shifting to a

customer-centric culture, as it helps mitigate resistance and ensures alignment.

5. **Chief Customer Officer (CCO)**
A senior executive responsible for overseeing and enhancing customer experience and success efforts. The CCO ensures that customer-centric strategies align with overall business goals.

6. **Customer Advocacy**
When customers actively support or recommend a company to others based on their positive experiences. Advocacy is often seen as a goal of excellent CX and CS, turning satisfied customers into brand ambassadors.

7. **Customer-Centric Culture**
An organizational mindset that prioritizes customer needs, satisfaction, and outcomes across all departments. Building a customer-centric culture requires alignment, leadership, and a commitment to continuous improvement.

8. **Customer-Centric Strategy**
A business strategy that places the customer at the center of all decisions, ensuring that the organization aligns its products, services, and experiences to meet customer expectations.

9. **Customer Churn**
The percentage of customers who stop using a

company's product or service within a given time period. High churn can indicate dissatisfaction, lack of engagement, or a competitive market.

10. **Customer Engagement**
The degree to which customers actively interact with a brand, product, or service. Engagement can include frequent product usage, social media interactions, and loyalty program participation, and it often indicates customer satisfaction.

11. **Customer Experience (CX)**
The sum of all interactions a customer has with a company, from initial awareness through the purchase process and beyond. It includes every touchpoint, whether digital, in-store, or through customer support, shaping the customer's perception of the brand.

12. **Customer Journey**
The complete set of experiences that a customer goes through when interacting with a company, from initial discovery to purchase, post-purchase support, and loyalty. Understanding the journey helps businesses identify critical touchpoints.

13. **Customer Lifetime Value (CLV)**
A prediction of the total revenue a company expects to earn from a customer over the entire duration of their relationship. CLV helps businesses

understand the long-term value of customer retention.

14. **Customer Retention**
    The ability of a company to retain customers over a specific period. Retention is often measured as a percentage of existing customers who remain loyal, and it is crucial for long-term growth.

15. **Customer Satisfaction (CSAT)**
    A metric that gauges how satisfied customers are with a company's products, services, or interactions. CSAT is typically measured by customer feedback, often through surveys after specific interactions.

16. **Customer Success (CS)**
    A proactive approach focused on helping customers achieve their desired outcomes when using a product or service. Customer Success ensures that customers derive value, receive support, and meet their goals, fostering a long-term relationship.

17. **Employee Experience (EX)**
    The overall experience and satisfaction employees have with their organization, from recruitment to exit. A positive EX is often linked to better CX, as satisfied employees are more likely to provide great service.

18. **Feedback Loop**
    A process for collecting, analyzing, and responding to customer feedback. A continuous feedback loop helps companies identify and address issues, improving CX and adapting to customer needs in real time.

19. **Functional Needs**
    The basic requirements customers have for a product or service. These include its ability to perform as expected and deliver core benefits. Fulfilling functional needs is the foundation of the Customer Hierarchy of Needs.

20. **Jacob Morgan**
    A bestselling author and futurist known for his work on Employee Experience and the future of work. Morgan's book, *The Employee Experience Advantage*, outlines the impact of a company's culture, technology, and workplace environment on employee satisfaction and productivity.

21. **Jobs-To-Be-Done (JTBD)**
    A theory in business and innovation that suggests customers "hire" products or services to perform specific tasks or solve particular problems. Understanding a customer's JTBD helps align CX and CS with their real goals.

22. **Key Performance Indicator (KPI)**
    A measurable value that demonstrates how

effectively a company is achieving specific objectives. In CX, common KPIs might include NPS, Customer Satisfaction (CSAT), and retention rates.

23. **Microsoft**
A multinational technology corporation known for its software products, cloud services, and devices. Microsoft's CEO Satya Nadella is noted for transforming the company's culture to be more customer-focused.

24. **Net Promoter Score (NPS)**
A customer loyalty metric based on the question, "How likely are you to recommend our company to a friend or colleague?" Responses are scored from 0-10 and categorized as Promoters (9-10), Passives (7-8), or Detractors (0-6). NPS is calculated by subtracting the percentage of Detractors from the percentage of Promoters.

25. **Onboarding**
The initial phase of a customer's journey after purchasing a product or service. Onboarding involves training, support, and resources to ensure the customer understands and effectively uses the product.

26. **Personalization**
The process of tailoring experiences, recommendations, or content to individual

customers based on their preferences, behavior, or previous interactions. Personalization enhances the customer experience by making it more relevant.

27. **Proactive Support**
A customer success strategy that anticipates and addresses customer needs before they escalate into problems. Proactive support fosters loyalty by reducing friction and enhancing customer satisfaction.

28. **Richard Branson**
The founder of the Virgin Group, Branson is known for his customer-centric approach and his belief in putting employees first. His philosophy is that taking care of employees leads to happier customers, which in turn benefits shareholders.

29. **Satya Nadella**
CEO of Microsoft who is recognized for leading a cultural shift within the company toward customer-centricity. Nadella emphasizes a "customer-obsessed" mindset, encouraging all executives to start discussions with the customer's needs in mind.

30. **Steve Jobs**
The co-founder of Apple, known for his visionary approach to product design and customer experience. Jobs' focus on simplicity, functionality,

and intuitive design has influenced countless customer-centric strategies in tech.

31. **Steve Wozniak**
The co-founder of Apple and an engineering genius who worked closely with Steve Jobs. Wozniak's technical expertise and attention to detail helped build products that are both reliable and innovative, contributing to Apple's reputation for quality.

32. **Touchpoint**
Any interaction or communication between a customer and a company. Touchpoints can include website visits, social media interactions, in-store experiences, customer service calls, and more.

33. **Virgin Group**
A British multinational conglomerate founded by Richard Branson, known for its diverse range of businesses and a customer-centric approach. Virgin Group's philosophy emphasizes exceptional customer service and employee satisfaction.

34. **Voice of the Customer (VoC)**
A collection of customer insights, feedback, and expectations gathered through various channels like surveys, interviews, and social media. VoC is essential for understanding customer needs and informing business decisions.

35. **Zappos**
   An online retailer known for its outstanding customer service and commitment to creating a memorable Customer Experience. Zappos has a philosophy of "wowing" the customer, going above and beyond to ensure customer satisfaction, and has become an iconic example of customer-centricity.

About the Author

Bibi Sofowote is a distinguished leader in the field of Customer Experience (CX), bringing over a decade of hands-on expertise to the conversation. As a thought leader, Bibi is known for demystifying the often overwhelming and jargon-filled landscape of Customer Experience. With an extensive background in the SaaS space where he has built and led award-winning teams, Bibi understands both the business dynamics and the customer perspective. This unique vantage point allows Bibi to break down complex industry terms in a way that resonates not only with professionals but also with anyone impacted by the evolution of service delivery in the digital age.

In *What the Actual Fuss: Why the CX Buzzword Is Relentlessly Haunting You,* Bibi tackles the growing frenzy around Customer Experience. This book cuts through the fluff and explores why the term "CX" has become a relentless buzzword, often overused without real substance.

With a mix of humor, critical insights, and a no-nonsense approach, Bibi calls attention to what truly makes or breaks customer relationships. This isn't just another CX guide; it's an eye-opener that dares readers to rethink the way they view customer interactions and the importance of genuine value in service. Through the pages, Bibi invites readers to understand the hype, confront the challenges, and, most importantly, redefine what Customer Experience should truly mean.

www.ingramcontent.com/pod-product-compliance
Lightning Source LLC
Chambersburg PA
CBHW071459220526
45472CB00003B/858